Stopping Time

A Rephotographic Survey of Lake Tahoe

Peter Goin

Essay by C. Elizabeth Raymond

Robert E. Blesse

University of New Mexico Press

Albuquerque

Library of Congress Cataloging-in-Publication Data

Goin, Peter, 1951–
Stopping time : a reprophotographic survey of Lake Tahoe /
Peter Goin ; essay by C. Elizabeth Raymond, Robert E. Blesse.
        p.   cm.
ISBN 0-8263-1284-5   ISBN 0-8263-1285-3 (pbk.)
1. Tahoe, Lake, Region (Calif. and Nev.)—Description and travel—Views.
2. Landscape—Tahoe, Lake, Region (Calif. and Nev.)
I. Raymond, C. Elizabeth.
II. Blesse, Robert E.
III. Title.
F868.T2G65   1992
979.4'38—dc20   91-29145
                                 CIP

Contents

Map of Lake Tahoe, 1873.

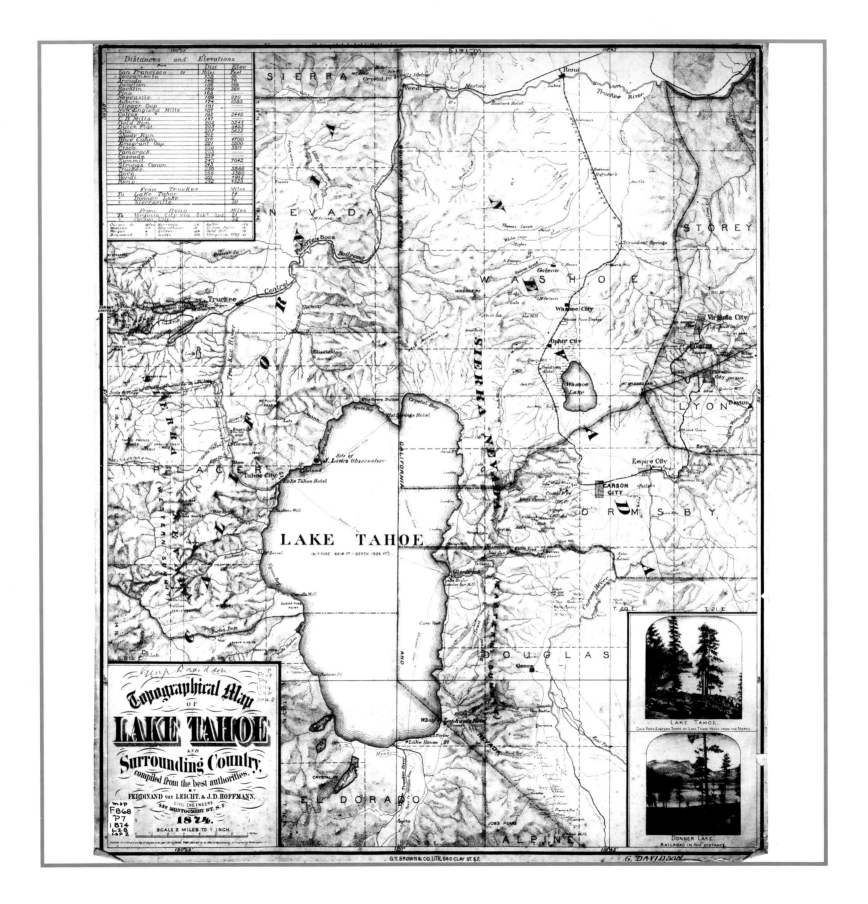

Topographical Map
OF
LAKE TAHOE
AND
Surrounding Country,
compiled from the best authorities,
BY
FERDINAND von LEICHT & J. D. HOFFMANN,
CIVIL ENGINEERS
432 MONTGOMERY ST. S.F.
1874.
SCALE 2 MILES TO 1 INCH.

LAKE TAHOE
(ALTITUDE 6216 FT - DEPTH 1525 FT.)

LAKE TAHOE.
CAVE ROCK, EASTERN SHORE OF LAKE TAHOE TAKEN FROM THE NORTH.

DONNER LAKE.
RAILROAD IN THE DISTANCE.

Map of Lake Tahoe, 1991.

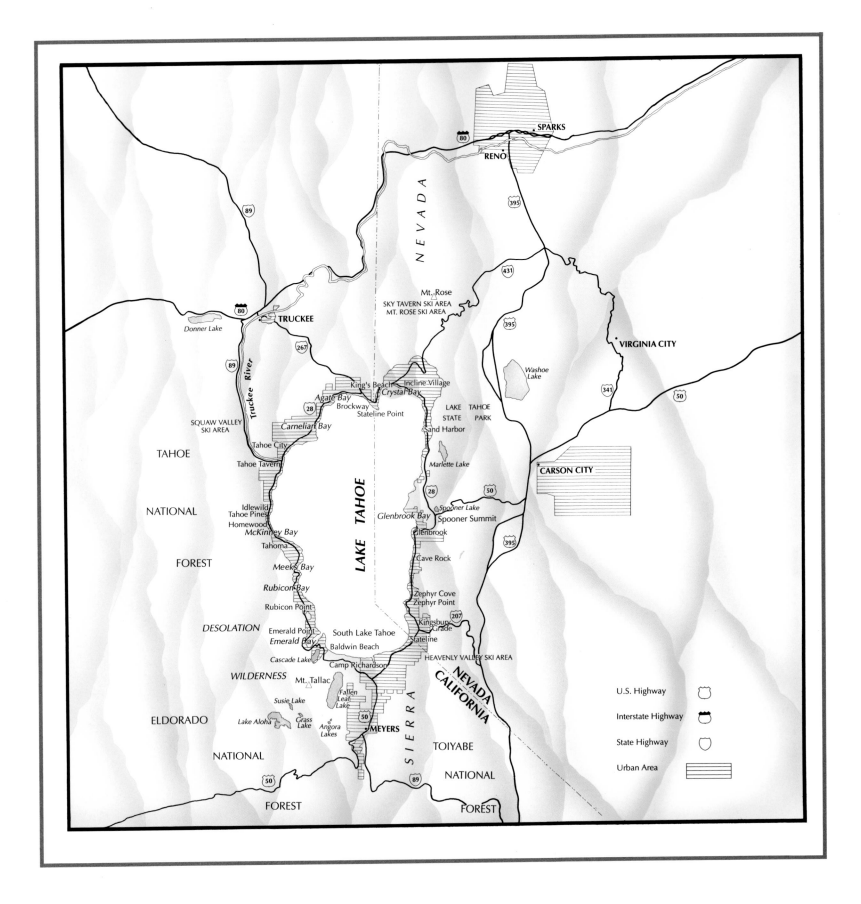

The Evolving Landscape at Lake Tahoe

Peter Goin

Lake Tahoe is one of America's most pristine, beautiful alpine lakes. Nestled in the Sierra Nevada at 6,229 feet above sea level, straddling the California-Nevada border, Lake Tahoe is renowned for its crystal clear water and scenic splendor. Surrounded by the Eldorado, Toiyabe, and Tahoe national forests, Lake Tahoe is one of the deepest lakes in North America—1,645 feet deep and covering 193 square miles. Currently supporting nearly 250,000 people, the watershed at Lake Tahoe provides nearly 85 percent of the water for northern Nevada and the Truckee-Donner area. Although some people perceive it simply as a reservoir, others are interested in capitalizing on its value as a tourist attraction. Golf courses, casinos, and skiing villages are signs of the area's tourist economy. Expensive homes and vacation retreats line the shores. Rapidly escalating property values testify to the demand for real estate. And as a testimony to its value as a resort, Lake Tahoe has been attracting more than eighteen million visitors each year.

The need to balance commercial growth with the preservation of Lake Tahoe as a natural, unspoiled environment creates problems that challenge the Tahoe basin's identity. Lake Tahoe is threatened by sewage and the effects of motorized boat traffic. Owing to five years of drought (1986–91), northern Nevada municipalities have seriously discussed proposals to drain Lake Tahoe below its natural rim. Dramatically over-harvested, Lake Tahoe's fish population has yet to return to its presettlement abundance. Ever-increasing demands for condominiums, vacation homes, and commercial structures endanger the fragile ecosystem. The hillsides are vulnerable to increasing erosion, sending greater amounts of soil and debris into the lake. The pressure to expand the Truckee-Tahoe Airport at South Lake Tahoe threatens to degrade the air and noise quality. Gaming is a growing industry. Roads encircle the Tahoe basin. Millions of visitors drive cars that contribute to the browning of Lake Tahoe's skies. Although logging is no longer a major industry, ski resorts clear downhill lanes through the second-growth forests. The construction of new dams has made the lakes in the Desolation Wilderness into reservoirs. Forest rangers talk about "campsite gridlock," where more hikers and campers visit the Desolation Wilderness than any other of the nation's 350 wilderness areas. In fact, the entire Tahoe landscape, at first accessible to only a few, has evolved from a remote mountain lake into a paradoxical urban/natural metropolis.

As this description suggests, Lake Tahoe suffers from many of the problems and challenges that threaten the western American landscape. The political, economic, and environmental issues that provoke debate about the future of Lake Tahoe reflect common problems that face many other communities. The conflict between environmental preservation and economic development has become a major American concern. Historically, economic development—mining, logging, ranching, farming, urban growth, access to markets, housing—has been a major determining factor in the creation of the American landscape. Yet the value of the landscape is not restricted to its economic potential. Natural environments also have aesthetic, even spiritual qualities. Whether the western landscape is understood and appreciated through the writings of John Muir, Frederick Law Olmstead, and Edward Abbey, for example, or through the photographs of Carleton Watkins and Ansel Adams, it is valued for its particular configuration of diverse natural qualities.

For many, the urban experience and the landscape experience are diametrically opposed. A sense of quiet and isolation are critical ingredients in how people seek to enjoy the wilderness. The sound of birds, the smell of the pine, the view of star-filled skies, and even the feel of the dirt become necessary components of such a restorative experience. Even if the wilderness is essentially managed and altered, the absence of urban elements such as cement, glass, cars, sirens, signs, and telephone wires becomes part of its essence.

Lake Tahoe's landscape, perhaps simply due to its geographic location in the arid West, contains the seed of this inevitable conflict. The evolution of the landscape has been controlled by a relative balance between economic development and scenic preservation. Over time, and in various ways, the Lake Tahoe basin has become a prototype of the managed landscape. During the 96th Congress, on December 19, 1980, a public law was passed approving the Tahoe Regional Planning Agency. This agency was charged with the responsibility to encourage the "wise use and conservation of the waters of Lake Tahoe and of the resources of the area." This act recognized both the unique environmental and ecological values of the Tahoe basin and the need to manage the region carefully through rules and regulations. The stated goal of the agency was to "insure the equilibrium between the region's natural endowment and its manmade environment."

❏   ❏   ❏   ❏

Stopping Time offers fifty-one pairs of photographs that provide comparative views documenting landscape change in Lake Tahoe, Donner Lake, and Truckee, California. This survey includes images rarely published and redefines these images within the context of a changing landscape. Quite simply, the historical photographs are rephotographed from nearly the same position in order to provide a comparison of landscape change.

Robert E. Blesse, a rare book and manuscript librarian, was responsible for finding the historical images used throughout the survey. The photographs date from the 1870s to the 1950s. Many thousands of photographs preserved in collections from the Seaver Center for Western History, the Nevada Historical Society, and the California Department of Transportation to the Sacramento History Center, the North Lake Tahoe Historical Society, and the Bancroft Library were reviewed for photographic quality, geographic distribution and representation, visual content, and uniqueness (compared to images commonly used to represent the Tahoe basin).

Lake Tahoe was not the subject of any of the major nineteenth-century surveys such as Lt. Wheeler's Survey of the Territory West of the 100th Meridian or Clarence King's U.S. Geological Exploration of the 40th Parallel. Few of the major nineteenth-century photographers visited Lake Tahoe, and if they did, their photographs generally celebrated the beauty of alpine sunsets. Recording topographical detail was rarely the photographic goal when confronted with Lake Tahoe's spectacular beauty. For example, Carleton Watkins made *A Storm on the Lake, Lake Tahoe* (c. 1873–78, Fig. 1) and stereo views showing the setting sun over a blackened horizon such as *Lake Tahoe, from the Warm Springs* (c. 1878, Fig. 2). During 1873, he received a commission to photograph the Carson and Tahoe Fluming Company's works at Glenbrook, but these photographs are an exception to Watkins's more prevalent idealized views. (Two Watkins photographs from the commissioned series are included in this survey. One photograph of the mill at Glenbrook was not chosen because the vantage point is now entirely hidden by trees. Two other anonymous photographs were used to convey the necessary comparative views. The commissioned photograph, *Upper End of Carson and Tahoe Lumber and Flume Co. Lumber and Wood Yard near Carson City*, c. 1873, falls outside of the geographic parameter of this survey.)

Many historical photographs—although made by commercial or moderately trained photographers—do not demonstrate the dynamic visual sensibility, technical skill, or intellect usually found in the works of photographers like Timothy O'Sullivan, Carleton Watkins, William Bell, or William Henry Jackson. The

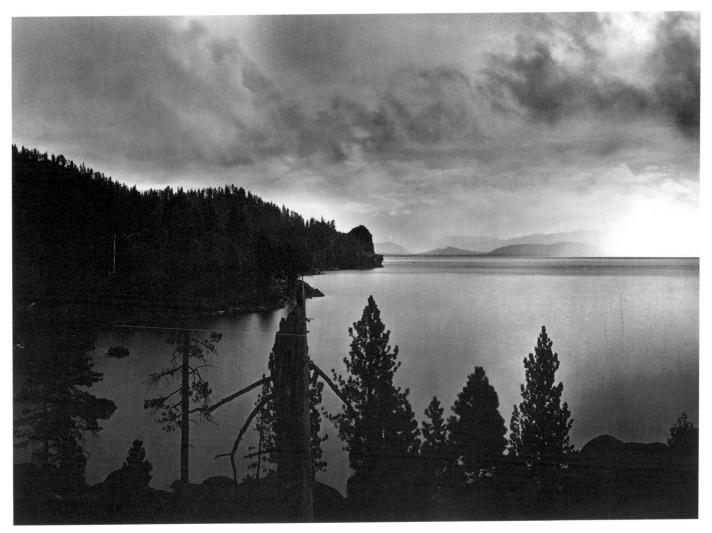

Figure 1. Carleton E. Watkins, *A Storm on the Lake, Lake Tahoe*, c. 1873–78.

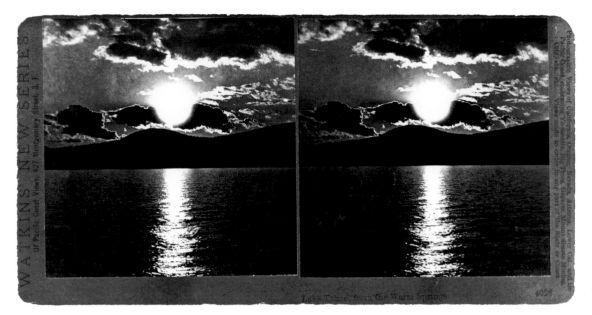

Figure 2. Carleton E. Watkins, *Lake Tahoe, from the Warm Springs,* c. 1878, print c. 1882.

vast majority of the photographs taken at Lake Tahoe in the last one hundred years represent the work of amateurs who used a diverse selection of cameras, lenses, film types, formats, and conceptual skill. Many archive photographs were rejected from this survey because of inferior quality: they were out-of-focus, too high or too low contrast, physically damaged, improperly printed, and/or poorly composed. In some cases, a photograph included in a collection had been copied from the original historical photograph, thus reducing its clarity and eliminating important information about the landscape. Others were selected, rephotographed, and rejected because they duplicated information contained in other photographs.

There have been, of course, Division of California Highway surveys, and lake-level surveys, but these photographs are limited in scope. For example, the highway survey photographs document the construction of the roadway. These images are important, and some are included, but they are not sufficient in themselves to represent the entire range of alteration of the Lake Tahoe landscape. Also, our perception of how that landscape changed is, to some degree, based simply upon the availability of historical photographs. Because photographers recorded the landscape selectively, the resource base for the survey is limited.

Why were some photographs made, and not others? In part, the characteristics of the landscape determined how many and what type of historical photographs were made. Before the lake was fully developed, some areas were not readily accessible. Most of Lake Tahoe's visitors in the mid-nineteenth century were viewing the lake for the first time and documenting their experience with photographs. The photograph became a visual "memory" of the landscape. These photographs were not intended to record the topographical characteristics of the landscape, since the study of how landscapes evolve was not a prevalent concern during the nineteenth and early twentieth centuries.

The technology of picture-making also changed radically during this period. Before the turn of the century, cameras were heavy, and the technical process of coating glass plates was difficult to master. The transportation network at the lake was in its infant stages, and using a tripod and large camera on a boat was problematic. Most early impressions of Lake Tahoe were recorded by visitors on boats.

Pure chance determined which photographs survived and are preserved, while others were abandoned or lost. After a detailed search, we discovered that the Tahoe landscape has never before been photographed in a systematic manner.

❏   ❏   ❏   ❏

Precise rephotography requires that the photographer use the exact same tripod position, camera format, lens and film type, and angle of view as well as the same time of day, year, and weather conditions. However, the degree of the landscape change at Lake Tahoe necessitated a flexible interpretation of the conventional rules governing precise rephotography.

The vantage—or tripod—position is predetermined by the historical photograph. Consequently, the site had to be identified, and a process of triangulation using foreground, middleground, background, and landmarks established the closest vantage point (vantage point is the lens's view). Although this project is a rephotographic survey, many of the paired photographs do not match exactly. The contemporary view may be taken from the same vantage point, using the same focal-length lens, camera, and film type, but in most cases, it is only close, not exact. Because the landscape has dramatically changed, many vantage points were eliminated. At Cave Rock, for example, the original vantage point no longer exists. The rock area where the photographer stood during the 1880s was later dynamited during the construction of the highway tunnel (Figs. 3 and 4).

Because the Tahoe basin was severely logged during the nineteenth and early twentieth centuries, the "best general view" was easily attainable. (The "best general view" describes the conceptual methodology used by many nineteenth-century photographers who sought to record the vast western landscape. Often this phrase was included in the title of a photograph,

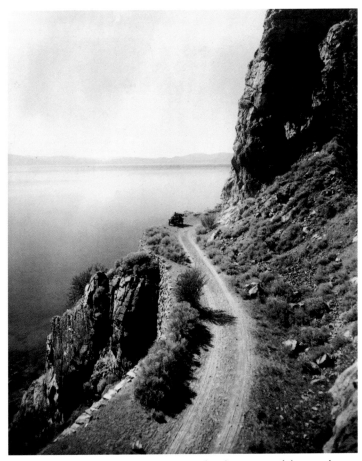

Figure 3. The original vantage point for this view of the road circumventing Cave Rock was located on rock and earth later excavated for the highway tunnel.

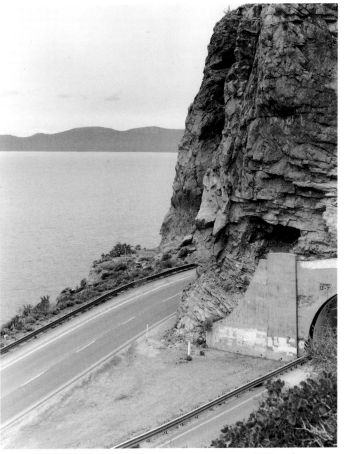

Figure 4. The rephotograph was made from the hill to the east of the current roadway.

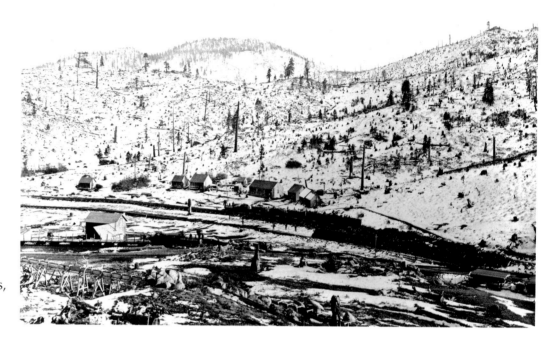

Figure 5. Spooner Summit. Carleton E. Watkins, *Junction of the Virginia and Truckee Railroad at Summit Wood Branch,* 1876.

reflecting the idea that a natural scene was best photographed from a specific vantage point.) The photographers could easily find vantage points that overlooked Glenbrook, South Lake Tahoe, or Tahoe City. Glenbrook, once a center for logging operations, was often photographed from the steep hills on the eastern shore of Lake Tahoe. These photographs provided compelling panoramic views of the surrounding area, including Shakespeare Rock, Glenbrook Bay, and Deadman Point. Now, however, the landscape has noticeably changed. The shore at Glenbrook Bay has dramatically receded, because the tons and tons of sawdust no longer clog and extend the natural beach (see pages 28 and 29). The second-growth forests have matured. Given the reduction of destructive logging, combined with the regrowth of the forests, the original "best general view" now reveals only trees and little else. Carleton Watkins's photograph *Junction of Virginia and Truckee Railroad at Summit Wood Branch* (1876) reveals the effects of dramatic and thorough logging. Today, however, the exact vantage point is completely obscured by the trees (see Figs. 5–9).

Quite a few historical views are almost impossible to find

because the forest obstructs any visual reference—the horizon or a prominent landmark—that one needs to find the original vantage point. Because of the historical importance of the timber industry at Lake Tahoe, it is important to include paired photographs of logging areas that accurately represent the nature of landscape change. This conflict—the goal of documenting significant change versus the inability to duplicate the exact vantage point—forced a reconsideration of the conventional rules governing rephotography.

At Tahoe, as elsewhere, land is constantly being manipulated in order to create the proper right-of-way for a paved roadway, or the slope necessary for a two-story cabin. In some cases, the historical photograph provided few, if any, clues to its location because it lacked a landmark or horizon, and a caption. If the site has been dramatically changed and the horizon has been obscured, only identifiable structures or the view can provide a clue to its location.

The problems in finding the exact camera position created a method of evaluating the landscape based upon intuition rather than science. In some cases, precise triangulation was possible.

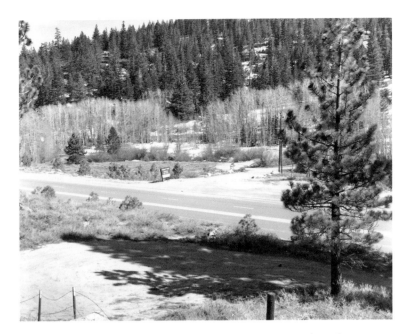

Figure 6. The vantage point for the Watkins photograph no longer offers a similar view owing to the second-growth forests. Consequently, the rephotograph had to be made from a clearing closer to the site of the railroad siding.

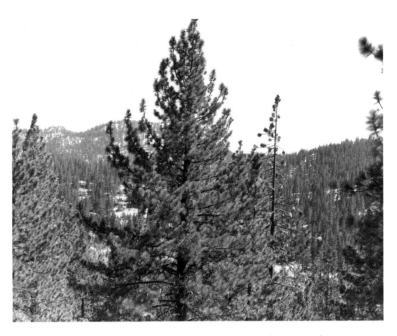

Figure 7. The vantage point for many historical photographs is verified by locating the appropriate horizon to foreground relationship. Although the horizon for the Watkins photograph is similar, the foreground is obscured.

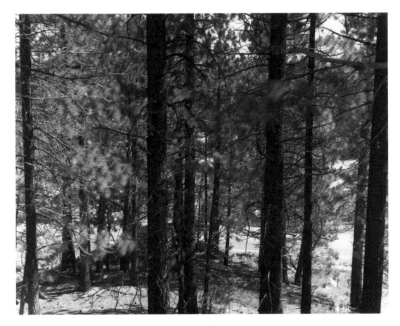

Figure 8. When the historical view is obscured, an analysis of the contour of the foreground can reveal the original photographer's vantage point. Although the trees significantly alter the view, it is still possible to estimate the location of the original tripod position.

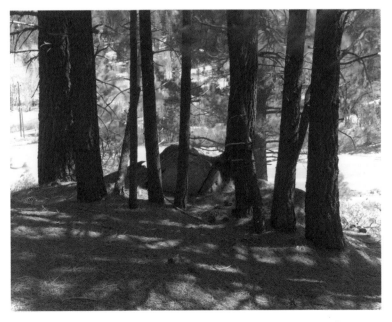

Figure 9. A close analysis of the rocks in this photograph verifies that these are the same rocks pictured in the foreground of the Watkins view.

But, as the preceding examples demonstrate, a general feel for the contour of the land was the only way to find the spot for an appropriate rephotograph. Intrinsic to the intuitive approach is the knowledge of the technology of earlier lenses, and of the effects of different focal-length lenses on how the landscape is depicted. Through wide-angle lenses, for example, the hills and mountains at the horizon will appear much smaller within the rectangle of the photograph. By contrast, a telephoto lens will compress the sense of space, creating the illusion that the background is much closer, larger, and more dominant than it actually is. Sometimes, instead of using the mountain-horizon relationship to the original vantage point, the contour of the foreground was the only reliable reference.

The comparison between two landscape photographs, made on the same hour and day and from the same vantage point exactly seventy or eighty years apart, provides a measure of the passage of time. Yet the landscape does not reflect the steady progress of the clock. Rather, time is measured by visual change in the landscape. Consequently, time passes at different rates, depending upon how many years separate the historical and contemporary views and the degree of change reflected at each site within the landscape. Recognizing the complexity of the concept of the time thus becomes increasingly important. Especially in the photographs taken within the Desolation Wilderness, it is interesting to notice how little landscape change has taken place within the last ninety or one hundred years. Except for the effect of the dam on the Aloha chain of lakes, the differences are relatively slight (see pages 66–73). Time passes relatively slowly within the wilderness, measured in rock fractures, lake levels, and tree growth. Within the Tahoe basin, however, the change is dramatic. Compare the pregaming photograph at Stateline (page 56) with the contemporary, high-rise casino urban area now dominating the landscape (page 57).

The concept of time is interpreted both as a measurement of landscape change and as an important element in the language of photography. Obviously, time controls the length of film exposure, dictating, for example, the role motion plays in the composition. But the position of the sun and the quality of the light have a strong influence on the composition of the photograph. Time and daylight are interwoven within the visual design of a photograph. Changing the composition can affect the viewer's interpretation and visceral response to the photograph. If this project

was specifically limited to the study of erosion patterns or geologic change, for example, then the role of light and shadow would necessarily be standardized to reflect the historical photograph. But the historical photographs in this survey were made for a variety of reasons, scientific analysis being the least prominent. Also, most of the photographs were made by amateurs who did not incorporate light as a significant element in the visual design. The shadows and patterns created by the angle of the sunlight were coincidental to the physical subject of the photograph. The photographs were not about visual design, and the formal qualities of light, angle, shape, and composition were rarely the primary subject of the photograph.

The fact that many historical photographs include passive elements of visual design encouraged our interpretation of their subject and content as raw data. The quality of a photograph depends on the skill of the photographer while the meaning of a photograph changes depending on how it is presented and seen. This survey places the historical photographs in a new context, changing the importance and meaning of the subject within the photograph. Even if a particular photographer sought to record his companion sitting in the car by the lakeshore, the photograph is valuable to this survey if it shows how the road was expanded, or the shoreline raised, or the rocks excavated. The original photographer's intent in making the photograph is subordinated to the material contained within it. The subject is appropriated to focus on the understanding and study of landscape change.

Rather than reproduce the historical views using the exact technical format, the contemporary photographs were made with vastly superior and standardized materials—80mm lens (645 format), 150mm and 210mm lens (4 × 5 format), panorama lens (Widelux), 125 ASA 4 × 5 film or 120 film, or Polaroid type 55 film. The historical formats were varied and diverse; this survey converts the historical material into a standard methodology, which may even inspire future rephotographic surveys.

❑   ❑   ❑   ❑

Photographs contain and reflect much more information than the record of light on paper. The attempt to reduce the contemporary photograph to an exact replica of the historical photograph denies the many technical, visual, and conceptual factors that influence our interpretation of the site being photographed. In the abstract, the most appropriate rephotograph of a nineteenth-century tourist picture would be a contemporary *tourist picture,* made at a similar vantage point—assuming that the "best general view" is still evident. This project would never have been completed if it depended upon the entirely random possibility such a suggestion demands.

The introduction of new variables partially obscuring the visual comparison is a conscious decision. As noted above, many of the historical photographs are technically inferior, with too much contrast, lost detail in the shadows, surface blemishes and scratches, poor focus, and design weaknesses. Creating a contemporary document that incorporated (and duplicated) those qualities seemed inappropriate. *Stopping Time* seeks to reinterpret the historical photographs by providing a contemporary example of a *similar* view. This project offers comparisons of vantage point and the perception of the landscape in two distinct yet similar photographs. The resulting pair transcends the particular criteria of each exposure. The meaning of each photograph is dependent upon the other.

Photographs are basically artifacts. But because each photograph (historical versus contemporary) represents a different conceptual premise, this project required flexibility in overcoming the limitations and differences incumbent in the historical material. The project seeks to convey a wide variety of ideas beyond what tree grew where, or what building burned down. For example, what is the connection between the photographic language and the concept of rephotography? How does the photograph convey information about landscape change?

The Lake Tahoe landscape is neither entirely natural nor completely urbanized. The term *landscape* includes the natural and human-made; landscape becomes architecture. Just as a building is laid upon a foundation, designed, raised, decorated, managed, and established as a functioning system, so the landscape at Lake Tahoe has become a human-altered and managed environment. The support required for the large mining activity at Virginia City, Nevada, denuded the landscape at Lake Tahoe, established many financial fortunes (reflected in property ownership at Lake Tahoe), and created an economic climate based on resource and tourist development. Lake Tahoe's intrinsic beauty was defined by its economic potential. The scenic splendor at Lake Tahoe and the notion that the area was a resort created a demand for the landscape. Landscape became real estate.

As society changed, so did the landscape at Lake Tahoe. During 1871, a dam was built to control the waters entering the Truckee River. This managed water system eventually provided the foundation for the tremendous growth of the Reno-Sparks metropolitan area. Lake Tahoe became a reservoir. The diversion of the Truckee River at Derby Dam and the Newlands Project (opened June 17, 1905) created an oasis of farming activity in the Fallon area. Winnemucca Lake, denied Truckee River water by that diversion, dried up, and a major stopping point for thousands of waterfowl on the Pacific Flyway was eliminated. During the 1930s, gambling was legalized in Nevada, and a bustling economy developed on the Nevada side of Lake Tahoe. The California-Nevada border line reflects the two state legal systems; in California, gaming is illegal. The introduction of regional, state, and protected wilderness areas affected the landscape, encouraging the regrowth of the forests. Building moratoriums have come and gone. Legislative bills have been introduced in both Nevada and California requesting public money be used to acquire "sensitive" lands within the Tahoe basin. Environmental impact statements are required before building permits will be granted. The Tahoe Regional Planning Agency requires a special permit for excavating more than seven cubic yards of soil. Adding decorative paving stones to a garden at Lake Tahoe requires a permit, because they add to a property's impervious ground cover. Fish populations are augmented by stocking the Desolation Wilderness lakes. Predators are monitored to keep wild animal populations in check. *Public access* is a modern term distinguishing the few shoreline areas that are not privately owned. Fences restrict free movement throughout the landscape.

The Lake Tahoe landscape is not "natural" in the traditional definition of the word; it is clearly and dramatically affected by human presence. The evolution of this modified "landscape as architecture" is the subject of this rephotographic survey.

Lake Tahoe has become many things to many people. To some, it represents a fortune in real estate. To others, it is an opportunity to seek out and discover the alpine experience. Whether Lake Tahoe is primarily a resort or a wilderness, it is increasingly clear that our collective role in the landscape is rarely passive. Nature at Lake Tahoe is firmly within human grasp.

"A Place One Never Tires Of": Changing Landscape and Image at Lake Tahoe[1]

C. Elizabeth Raymond

When John Frémont became the first white man to sight the lake now known as Tahoe, on a misty day in February 1844, his description of it was laconic. In his journals he noted simply that he and his surveyor had ascended a mountain "from which we had a beautiful view of a mountain lake at our feet, about fifteen miles in length, and so entirely surrounded by mountains that we could not discover an outlet."[2] Frémont and his party never did discover Tahoe's only outlet, the Truckee River at the northwestern corner of the lake. Instead they were soon on their way again, leaving the isolated mountain lake undisturbed. For a few more years the principal visitors were members of the local Washoe tribe, who migrated to Tahoe from nearby Nevada valleys annually in June. They remained through early autumn at various sites in the basin, fishing, hunting, and gathering plants for food and reeds for baskets. During mild winters, some Washoe families even remained at the lake year round.[3]

Frémont's 1844 visit, however, was the harbinger of a much greater white intrusion—as well as many more poetic descriptions—in the years to come. Lake Tahoe rapidly became renowned after the 1848 discovery of gold in California, and the identification eleven years later of Nevada's rich Comstock Silver Lode.[4] The 1860s rush east from California's gold fields to the new silver mines in "Washoe," took place along Lake Tahoe's

shores. Ranchers and hostlers moved in to take advantage of this suddenly populous location. A brief mining boom in Squaw Valley in 1863 brought miners virtually to the shores of the lake itself, and although the boom quickly collapsed, some permanent settlers remained behind. The phenomenal growth of Virginia City, Nevada, to the east, further spurred development of the Lake Tahoe basin, which supplied both water and wood for the new community.

The nature and impact of that development is the subject of the present collection of photographs. As a group, they dramatically register the physical consequences of the transformation of the Tahoe landscape at intervals over approximately 120 years. Yet those physical changes are only part of the story, because prevailing attitudes toward Lake Tahoe also evolved during this same period. Images of the lake—what it meant to those who visited it—have also varied remarkably over those same 120 years.

In the mid-nineteenth century the lake was most often assessed primarily in terms of its economic promise. Changes that would be deplored today, such as clear-cutting the slopes for timber, were acclaimed by a nineteenth-century society that celebrated human dominion over nature. Only later, as the preservation ethos promoted by John Muir and others began to spread, did that value system shift to promote protection rather than exploitation of the landscape. In the twentieth century, there were several unsuccessful attempts to create a national park at Tahoe. Certain groups, however, continued to view the landscape in terms of its economic potential. The difference was that tourism, rather than timber, became the principal industry, so that protection, rather than extraction of natural resources, became the watchword. In the twentieth century, land use at Tahoe began to be assessed in terms of its potential negative impact on the scenery. Such changes in attitudes, in the ways the lake was seen and understood by contemporaries, shaped a perceptual world that in turn permitted or censured certain physical developments in the region.

The physical alteration of the Tahoe landscape has been extensive, as the photographs demonstrate. The modern terrain is an artifact, created by almost 150 years of active human intervention in the basin. Images have also played a role in the process, however, because the different ways that people have viewed nature at Tahoe have inevitably affected their environmental choices. This essay will explore both kinds of change, in the actual Tahoe landscape, and in the historical perception of it. Understanding both the physical development and the various images generated by travelers, reporters, guidebooks, and other writers will provide a context for viewing the specific environmental transmutations depicted in the photographic pairs.

Shortly after Frémont's visit, the Washoe began to have competition for the plentiful resources of the Tahoe basin. The first log cabin was built at Tahoe in 1851, and by 1854 a permanent trading post was located on the wagon road that went east from Sacramento along the south end of the lake through Luther Pass. Stagecoaches were traveling the latter route by 1857, and a toll road was built down Kingsbury Grade to Genoa, Nevada, by 1860. The discovery and growth of Virginia City enticed thousands of eager fortune-seekers from California along these roads, along with hundreds of freight wagons loaded with supplies for the new mining center. Inns and lodging stations sprang up to minister to them, and a few ranchers undertook to supply the animals with hay. A small sawmill was established in 1861 at Glenbrook, on the Nevada shore, to supply much-needed lumber to the growing communities. A hotel was added in 1863, to serve the travelers along the toll road from Placerville to Genoa.

In that same year, gold was discovered in Squaw Valley, California, about five miles northwest of the lake. Some 600 hopeful miners flocked to the camps of Knoxville and Claraville, which disappeared just as rapidly as they had sprung up, when the strike proved illusory. Some of those who stayed behind, however, followed the Truckee upstream and established Tahoe City, California, in 1864, at the outlet from Lake Tahoe. These two settlements, at Tahoe City in California and Glenbrook in Nevada, remained the population centers of the basin for the remainder of the century. By 1864, a small excursion steamer, the *Governor Blaisdel,* was operating to connect the two.

All this development brought greater public attention to the region, and to the mountain lake at its heart. Large groups of would-be silver miners traveled back and forth across the basin on their way to Nevada. Along the way they commented admiringly, as did J. Ross Browne in 1864, on the lake then generally known as Bigler, after a popular governor of California. Browne viewed the lake from the wagon road and didn't bother to detour down to its shores, but he noted its majestic position "embosomed in the mountains" and observed that he had "seldom witnessed any scene in Europe or elsewhere to compare with it in extent or grandeur."[5] In a long and miserable trip to and from the new mines in Virginia City, Tahoe was literally the only thing that Browne found to admire.

Browne was not alone in his favorable comments. As early as 1859, the San Francisco newspapers were printing accounts of Tahoe which described it as a virtual paradise. The *Alta California* reprinted an item from Nevada's *Genoa Enterprise,* which chronicled most of the features of the lake that would continue to be extolled by generations of tourists: bracing elevation, color and purity of the water, beauty of situation, and plentiful fishing. Even at this early date, the correspondent expressed confidence that Tahoe would soon become a byword, "beyond all doubt naturally one of the most interesting and agreeable resorts for pleasure and amusement on the borders of the Pacific."[6] In 1859, there were no boats on the lake, nor were there pleasure resorts for the anticipated tourists, but both the accommodations and the tourists would appear in short order.

Meanwhile, the lake's name continued to be a matter of confusion for several years. The name *Tahoe,* derived from a Washoe word signifying "lake," was first applied in 1862. Frémont had originally called it Bonpland, and it had appeared on some maps as Mountain Lake. It began to be called Bigler in 1853, after the popular California governor helped rescue a party from its eastern shore. A new designation was thought necessary in some quarters, however, when Bigler supported the Confederacy in the Civil War.[7] Although the California legislature officially named the lake Bigler in 1870, Tahoe remained the most common appellation. In 1945, belatedly succumbing to the inevitable, the California legislature officially adopted the name Tahoe for the lake.[8]

So it was known to young Samuel Clemens when he made his famous trip to the lake in 1861, while serving as personal secretary to his brother Orion, the territorial secretary for Nevada. As chronicled later in *Roughing It,* Clemens walked from Carson City to Tahoe with his friend Johnny K. After grumbling that the eleven-mile trip seemed longer than expected, they were stunned by their first sight of the lake. In what is probably the quintessential description of Tahoe, Clemens waxed uncharacteristically poetic:

> . . . at last the Lake burst upon us—a noble sheet of blue water lifted six thousand three hundred feet above the level of the sea, and walled in by a rim of snow-clad mountain peaks that towered aloft full three thousand feet higher still! . . . As it lay there with the shadows of the mountains brilliantly photographed upon its still surface I thought it must surely be the fairest picture the whole earth affords.

Their subsequent misadventures, as they first staked a 300-acre timber claim near Carnelian Bay and then helplessly watched their newfound fortune literally go up in smoke when a cooking fire inadvertently consumed the entire mountainside, were ruefully recounted by a chastened Clemens. But there was no irony in his breathless descriptions of the lake's beauty: "The view was always fascinating, bewitching, entrancing. The eye was never tired of gazing, night or day, in calm or storm; it suffered but one grief, and that was that it could not look always, but must close sometimes in sleep." Like other observers both before and since, Sam Clemens was astounded by the beauty of Lake Tahoe.[9]

Yet beauty was not the only appeal of the mountain lake, as Clemens's misadventure suggests. A strong economic motive also attracted attention to the Tahoe basin in the late nineteenth century, and the very same people who lyrically extolled its resplendence also pragmatically tallied its potential assets. These became more valuable with increased accessibility. In 1868, the Central Pacific Railroad was being built through the Sierra

Nevada, and a station was established at Truckee, California, where the route intersected the river of the same name. With the development of more efficient transportation systems linked to the railroad, large-scale economic development of the Lake Tahoe basin began in the 1870s.

Nature had endowed Tahoe with substantial assets to be exploited. The lake itself was a giant reservoir in the midst of a desert. It was surrounded by enormous stands of timber in a generally treeless land, adjacent to both a mining area and a railroad, each of which had an insatiable appetite for wood. And finally, as the 1859 *Alta California* correspondent had presciently suggested, the beauty of its setting and its recreational potential made it a guaranteed tourist attraction. With the arrival of the railroad, each facet of Tahoe's economic potential began to be explored.

In 1870, a timber and stone crib dam was installed at the outlet of the Truckee by Alexander von Schmidt.[10] This ambitious engineer sought to store Tahoe water for shipment to San Francisco by means of a combination railroad tunnel and aqueduct through the Sierra Nevada. His plan was denounced by Nevada newspapers, which claimed that Tahoe water ought to be used in their perpetually thirsty state. Ultimately the plan never found the necessary financial support in San Francisco, despite a variety of promotional schemes. Nonetheless, faith in the lake's promise as a source of water continued high. As one guidebook summarized the matter in 1883:

> Years ago loud cries went up against the use of the water of Tahoe for municipal purposes. . . . The objection becomes supremely ridiculous when the many resources of supply for the lake are seen. . . . More water runs out of the lake each day and goes to waste than would be sufficient to supply New York, with its million inhabitants, with Brooklyn and Jersey City thrown in. The idea of depleting this lake is a farce.[11]

Eventually Central Pacific Railroad interests acquired the dam and operated it in order to ensure sufficient downstream flow to float logs to their mills at Truckee and elsewhere. Nevertheless, the issue of water storage at Lake Tahoe continued to be a matter for discussion, pitting potential downstream users, including powerful electric companies and lumber companies, against property owners at the lake who sought to protect themselves against the devastating effects of a fluctuating lake level. The Pyramid Lake Paiute Tribe consistently sought to prevent shrinkage of its principal fishery, Pyramid Lake, which was the natural terminus of the Truckee River. Finally, the states of California and Nevada, in which the lake was located, continually quarreled about their respective rights to its water.

The original dam at the river outlet was eventually replaced by a modern concrete structure in 1913, after the site had been acquired by a consortium of electric companies. They sought to regulate the lake level in order to ensure sufficient river flow to generate power even at times of low water. When Derby Dam was completed in Nevada in 1905, it drew water for the agricultural Newlands Project, near Fallon, Nevada, from the Truckee River. Thereafter the Bureau of Reclamation also had an interest in Tahoe water, as it sought to guarantee a steady supply of water to irrigate the desert crops. Several times in the twentieth century, during times of extreme drought, Nevada farmers threatened to dynamite the lake rim in order to seize the water they depended upon. In 1930, a steam shovel was actually sent to the lake, when the Truckee River stopped flowing, and emergency pumping was allowed in that year as in several others.

In 1934, the various parties finally reached a tentative agreement about disposition of Tahoe water. This agreement limited the fluctuation in lake level to six feet, from the natural outlet elevation of 6,223 feet, to no more than 6,229 feet. It also prohibited cutting of the rim and gave permission for the power company and the federal government to build storage reservoirs elsewhere on the Truckee. The agreement was confirmed by a federal court decree in 1944, although vexing questions about the division and disposition of Truckee River water among numerous interested parties still remain to be settled in 1991.

As the present, complicated arrangements for using Lake Tahoe water would suggest, its status as a reservoir has tremendous importance for the surrounding area. This is increasingly true in recent years, with exponential population growth both in the basin itself and in the downstream Nevada communities which depend on water from the Truckee River. Although von Schmidt's original vision of the lake as a municipal water supply for San Francisco proved illusory, Tahoe *has* become a crucial source of water for a substantial desert community of various groups with myriad different, and occasionally conflicting, plans for its use.

Tahoe's second major economic asset was wood, in the form of hundreds of thousands of acres of untouched timber on the surrounding mountain slopes. It was this resource, ripe for the harvesting, that initially attracted Sam Clemens to the lake in the early 1860s. A small sawmill was in operation at the south end of the lake as early as 1860, and another at Glenbrook in 1861. However, efficient, large-scale lumbering in the basin began only after invention in 1867 of the V-flume system for transporting wood to staging areas and the arrival in 1868 of the railroad.[12] Before that time, lumber was transported to the burgeoning market at Virginia City by wagon. This entailed hauling it up over the mountains and down to Carson City, then up again over the next range of hills into Virginia City. The V-flume and the railroad both made it less expensive to transport wood, the former by relying on water and gravity to float mill products down the mountains into Carson City, and the latter by easily carrying heavy loads of timber. In addition, the railroad also consumed vast amounts of wood to run its engines.

As demand for wood increased, systematic lumbering was initiated with the formation in 1873 of the Carson and Tahoe Lumber and Fluming Company. This company, owned by two executives of Virginia City's narrow-gauge railroad, the Virginia and Truckee, along with banker Duane L. Bliss, bought and vastly expanded the existing mills at Glenbrook. Eventually it owned or leased more than 50,000 acres in the Tahoe basin. In 1875, it constructed a narrow-gauge railroad to move wood 1,200 feet up the mountain from its Glenbrook mills east to Spooner Summit. From there a twelve-mile flume took the cordwood and timbers down into Carson Valley, where they could be moved again by the Virginia and Truckee Railroad to the mines at Virginia City. As the Virginia City mines entered the Big Bonanza period of the 1870s, and the city rebuilt after the disastrous fire of 1875, the demand for lumber continued to grow, and the Carson and Tahoe Lumber and Fluming Company responded by extending its operations around the lake. Trees were cut at various locations, hurled down dry log chutes to the lake, then gathered together into booms and hauled by steamer across the water to the mills at Glenbrook. There they were sawed and carried by railroad and flume to Carson Valley and then to Virginia City.[13]

While the Glenbrook operation was by far the largest at Tahoe, it was not the only one. Logging operations of various sizes operated throughout the region, including one at Incline, built by Walter S. Hobart and the Sierra Nevada Wood and Lumber Company. In 1880, Hobart's company completed a cable tramway that hauled its lumber up 4,000 feet from the mill to the summit, where it was transferred to a V-flume for the trip downhill to Washoe Valley. Other, smaller companies worked on contract, cutting trees and delivering them to the large mills for processing.

The result of this intensive lumbering was the virtual deforestation of large portions of the Tahoe basin by the 1890s. The Carson and Tahoe Lumber and Fluming Company closed its Glenbrook mills for lack of wood in 1898. Hobart's Sierra Nevada Wood and Lumber Company's last major operating season was 1894, and its reserves were depleted by 1897. Once flourishing, the two Nevada settlements built around these mills were both rapidly depopulated. The equipment at Incline was removed north and west to a new operation at Hobart Mills, and the post office was closed. Glenbrook's railroad was dismantled and consolidated with another company-owned logging railroad from the south shore of the lake to build a new road connecting the Southern Pacific Railroad at Truckee with the lake shore at Tahoe City. Opening of this new railroad along the banks of the Truckee River in 1900 marked the close of the lumbering era at Tahoe and a decisive shift toward cultivating tourism as the region's principal economic resource.

In its wake, the lumber industry left a drastically altered landscape. Most of the old growth forest was gone, replaced by open hillsides littered with slash and sawdust-choked creeks and rivers. Clear-cutting of the slopes, according to a 1900 forester's report, had retarded or entirely prevented reproduction of the supposedly renewable resource of timber: "With the subsequent ravages of fire, some cut-over lands have remained in a denuded state for many years and are still in this condition."[14] Most forest surfaces were bare of protective vegetation, due in part to over-grazing by itinerant sheep bands that used the basin lands for summer forage. Replacement forests, which were only ten to twenty feet high by the early twentieth century, tended to be white fir and yellow pine, instead of the more valuable sugar pine, which was slower to reproduce.[15] The new forests were vulnerable to fire because of the abundance of slash on the ground and the denseness of their growth. The landscape that the lumber companies deserted was an exhausted one, "shorn of its wealth and beauty," in the words of one contemporary observer.[16] With the exception of the 1899 Lake Tahoe Forest Reserve, and some acreage on the north shore of the lake and around Tallac, Tahoe was virtually logged out.

Despite the depletion of this important resource, interest in Tahoe did not diminish. Indeed, the exhaustion of Tahoe's timber only served to increase the importance of a previously secondary economic resource, the lake's recreational potential. Tourism at the lake was nothing new. Scenic spots had been catalogued, and tourists catered to, at least since the 1860s. But with the symbolic rededication of the Carson and Tahoe Lumber and Fluming Company's railroad, from hauling logs at Glenbrook to carrying tourists to Tahoe City, a new era of intensive economic exploitation of scenery had begun. This shift, too, had profound consequences for Tahoe's landscape.

Lake Tahoe had been depicted as a tourist destination almost from the moment of its discovery. A writer for the *Sacramento Union* listed its attractions in 1862:

> This lake, being in a direct line between Sacramento and Carson, the Capitals of California and Nevada, and easily made accessible by good roads, must soon become the Summer resort of the wearied man of business and the seeker after pleasure. The locality seems to have all the elements which serve to make up a good watering place—pure air, pure water, cool nights, freedom from noxious insects or reptiles, fine trees, fine cascades, clear gurgling brooks, running over white and pebbles, picturesque rocks, good fish and easily caught, fine sailing, fine rowing. All that is now wanted is a few good hotels and boardinghouses, which will no doubt come along in their proper time.[17]

True to this prediction, the tourist accommodations did arrive. Once the railroad replaced the wagon routes as the most popular means of access to Virginia City, the old freight roads began to be abandoned. The boardinghouses and way stations that had catered to those who joined the rush to Washoe were bypassed, and replaced by resort hotels closer to the lake. Among the most popular of these early resorts were Yank's Station at Meyers, Lake House at Al Tahoe, and Glenbrook House, established in 1864 at Glenbrook. The latter was renowned as the most luxurious hotel on the lake until the construction in 1871 of the Grand Hotel at Tahoe City.

As had been the case for timber, the railroad also abetted the growth of the tourist industry. When an intrepid newspaper reporter made the journey in 1864, he duly reported that "it's a mere holiday trip now to Lake Tahoe," requiring "but twenty hours' travel from San Francisco."[18] As soon as the railroad was completed, however, the trip was cut to nine hours, albeit with an overnight stay at Truckee.[19] Most tourists reached the lake at Tahoe City, by way of the Truckee River canyon from Truckee. Until the Carson and Tahoe Lumber and Fluming Company's Lake Tahoe Railway began operation in 1900, the trip was made by carriage or by wagon, with guidebooks recommending the latter, despite its discomforts, "as [the route] affords such commanding views of scenery that people are not disposed to complain of hard seats and a lack of springs."[20]

Once arrived at the lake, they took to the water. Most of the nineteenth-century roads in the basin were freighting and logging routes, not necessarily suitable for the tourist's itinerary. As logging areas were abandoned, these roads fell into disrepair, and no roads had ever connected the north and south shore in the nineteenth century. Instead the traveler was served by a variety of charter and scheduled sailboats and steamers, beginning with the tiny *Governor Blaisdel* in 1864, succeeded in turn by the *Governor Stanford* in 1873, the *Tallac* in 1890, and finally by the luxurious *Tahoe*, launched at Glenbrook in 1896 by the Bliss family. The *Governor Stanford* and the *Tahoe* followed regular schedules, meeting incoming carriages and later trains at Tahoe City and proceeding around the lake to make major stops at Brockaway, Carnelian Bay, Emerald Bay, Tallac, and Glenbrook, among others. They carried mail and freight as well as passengers, until growing automobile traffic and improvements in the roads rendered them obsolete. The *Tahoe* stopped its scheduled runs in 1935, and was scuttled by the Bliss family in 1940.[21] Until the coming of the automobile, however, and the improvement in Tahoe roads, the tourist's typical experience of the lake was from the water looking up at the shore, rather than from the road, looking out toward the lake.

This spectator's perspective was typical of most nineteenth-century tourists' accounts of Tahoe, which commonly described the lake as seen from a boat or a carriage, and recounted passive impressions rather than activities. Like Sam Clemens in *Roughing It*, most visitors found the lake a wonderful place for doing nothing. Laziness was the prevailing order of the day—apprehending instead of doing—as in one 1881 novel set at Tahoe: ". . . to enjoy Tahoe to the fullest extent, to revel amid her various beauties, and look at once upon her grandeur, we must float out upon her still transparent bosom, in a little boat, and give the mind time for its feastings."[22] In the nineteenth century, as historian John Sears has pointed out, tourism had an important cultural role in shaping American national identity. People visited famed natural sites as if they were shrines, where solemn reflection and adoration were the prescribed responses. In this regard, Tahoe was no exception. Nineteenth-century tourists came to the lake to experience its restorative powers, to see its sights, and to be spiritually uplifted amidst its well-known beauties.[23]

To do so, however, they required comfortable surroundings. As the lake grew in popularity, elegant resorts multiplied, including the notable Tallac, built by E. J. "Lucky" Baldwin in 1899, on land he had begun to purchase and protect from logging in 1878. This hotel consciously catered to the elite with steam heat, electric lights, piped water, picture windows, elaborate cuisine, and elegant amusements. In 1902, Baldwin added a casino that featured slot machines as well as dancing, but the entire complex was razed by his daughter in 1927, in favor of a private estate.[24] Most spectacular was the Bliss family's Tahoe Tavern, built in 1901 to serve the tourists deposited at Tahoe City by their new Lake Tahoe Railway. The Tavern, as it was familiarly known, combined sumptuous appointments similar to those of the Tallac with studied rusticity of design. Guests arrived there to stay for extended periods, to stroll the grounds and enjoy the ambience of a place that provided "exquisite glimpses of the dazzling blue of the water from every hand."[25] The Tahoe Tavern continued to operate until it was demolished in 1964.

For most of the nineteenth century, Lake Tahoe was a summer resort. Although some individuals wintered at the lake as the Washoe had done, most residents and tourists alike departed when the snow came. The Lake Tahoe Railway generally operated from May 15 to November 15 annually, and most hotels closed during the winter months.[26] Given the prevailing style of tourism in the nineteenth century, this was understandable. Gazing from an open boat or veranda at the changing colors of the sunset reflected in the lake waters held few attractions in the winter.

Yet, by the late nineteenth century, notions of leisure were changing, and new, more active styles of recreation replaced the older, sanitarium image at Tahoe. In 1911, one writer explicitly described the changes, noting that the annual vacation is now a custom, but that the hotel has become "secondary," serving "simply as a base from which to enjoy attractions beyond the power of architect and expert host to create." These attractions must involve physical activity in nature: "The present-day rest-seeker loses the old idea of vacation, 'a period of being unoccupied'; he wants varied occupations, something different from his usual employment but something that will occupy his active twentieth-century mind at the same time it is renewing his physical vigor."[27]

As more people began to enjoy Tahoe by actively hiking and traveling around its mountainous terrain, winter began to exercise a new appeal. As early as 1878, outdoor enthusiast John Muir extolled the lake as a winter destination, and an 1871 railroad guidebook noted that Tahoe featured winter sleighing, which was difficult to find west of the Rocky Mountains.[28] The region's increasing popularity as a winter destination was confidently predicted by Charles Howard Shinn in 1891, and an 1886 woodcut from *Mining and Scientific Press* depicted ski racing in the Sierra.[29]

It was the woodcut which most accurately forecast the future. Gradually, in the twentieth century, skiing became an important facet of Tahoe's attraction, and a permanent, year-round community grew up to take advantage of it. The Southern Pacific Railroad purchased the Lake Tahoe Railway and converted it to broad-gauge in 1926. In 1932, the railroad began operating "snowball special" ski trains to bring would-be skiers to Tahoe, following a precedent set earlier in the century, when people came by train to ice skate at Donner Lake, east of Truckee on the Southern Pacific Railroad's main line.[30] Tahoe Tavern sponsored a winter sports festival in 1928, and a ski-jumping tournament was staged at North Tahoe in 1930. One of the lake's oldest ski areas, Granlibakken, was a site for trials for the 1932 Winter Olympics, but the Tahoe basin became permanently and prominently identified with skiing only after 1955, when it was announced that the 1960 Winter Olympics would be held at Squaw Valley.[31] From then on, ski resorts multiplied, assisted by a policy of year-round maintenance for new and better roads into the region.

The state of California had authorized the survey of new roads over Echo Summit in 1895, and over Donner Summit in 1909. As automobile ownership increased, road building became crucial. By 1924, paved highways began to compete with the railroads at Tahoe, and by 1935 a passable auto route had been completed all the way around the lake.[32] Easy automobile access to the Tahoe basin changed the nature of tourism, as well. Buses and automobiles were more flexible than railroads. They could go to more places and carry fewer people economically. They made Lake Tahoe accessible to more people. At the same time they competed with the railroads and boats for lake traffic, with the result that both the Lake Tahoe Railway and the steamer *Tahoe* ceased operations by World War II. Automobile tourists tended to come for shorter periods of time and to seek less luxurious accommodations than their nineteenth-century predecessors. Their presence stimulated the establishment of new resorts and auto camps to serve their needs, such as Camp Richardson. In 1923, Alonzo Richardson purchased the former Gardner's resort property, added small rustic cabins and a pier, and began daily Pierce-Arrow auto stage trips between Tallac and Placerville, California. Camp Richardson's accessibility, relaxed atmosphere, and the addition of a gas station in the late 1920s, made it popular with middle-class families.[33]

By the 1930s, these changes had significantly altered the rhythm of Tahoe's tourist economy, and a small year-round settlement had grown up at the south end of the lake. The real winter boom at Tahoe, however, was launched by winter clearing of the access roads, which was authorized by California during World War II, but not reliably accomplished by either state until after the war. Combined with the 1960 Winter Olympics, opening of the Tahoe airport in 1959, and large new planned developments at Incline Village and Tahoe Keys in the 1960s, this not only facilitated a substantial year-round population but also attracted more winter tourists to the growing numbers of ski slopes.[34]

The final factor in transforming the Tahoe basin from a seasonal resort to the present year-round community of approximately 50,000 was gambling. Legalized by the state of Nevada in 1931, gambling in various forms had long been available at locations in both states around Tahoe. Most notable among these were Tallac, the Nevada Club at the south shore, and the Cal-Neva at Crystal Bay. The latter resort was purchased in 1930 by two of Reno's most notorious underworld figures, William Graham and James McKay. The Cal-Neva had been built on the state line and featured casino-style gambling and readily available alcohol, in spite of prohibition laws.[35] It was frequented by affluent Reno divorcees waiting out the three-month stay then necessary to establish Nevada residency. These early casinos had a limited clientele. With legalization, however, gambling became a significant industry in Nevada, and quickly expanded at Lake Tahoe as well.

Harvey and Llewellyn Gross established the first legal casino at what became Stateline, Nevada, in 1944, when they expanded their gas station into Harvey's Wagon Wheel Saloon and Gambling Hall. Despite slow winters in the early years, their operation survived and prospered, and they eventually built the first high-rise hotel-casino at Lake Tahoe, which opened in 1965. Their success drew attention to Stateline, and Harvey's was subsequently joined by several other casinos, including Harrah's in 1956. Harrah's round-the-clock operation, especially, contributed to the rapid growth of business at Stateline, which in turn brought large, permanent work forces and increased the permanent population at Tahoe. Harrah's began offering big-name entertainment at the lake in 1959, and all of the casinos devoted large advertising budgets to promoting Stateline as a year-round destination and providing "gamblers' special" chartered bus tours. With increased leisure time and easier access to the Lake Tahoe basin, hundreds of thousands of Californians responded eagerly to these blandishments. By the end of the 1950s, the south shore casinos had outdistanced the more established clubs on Tahoe's north shore.[36]

Thus, by the end of the twentieth century, tourism in various guises had become Tahoe's principal economic asset. Paradoxically, however, the boom had also produced a host of new difficulties, in their own ways as disturbing and disrupting as the conflicts over how and where to use the water, or the physical devastation of the lumbering. Tahoe in the twentieth century has come to be dominated economically by a tourism industry that depends directly on the landscape. Yet that landscape is increasingly imperiled by its own success, by the environmental pressures of large numbers of tourists, and the growing permanent population that exists at least in part to supply them.

As the population in the Tahoe basin has grown, sewage disposal has become a problem. The renowned clarity of the lake has decreased markedly as a result of run-off from sloping shores disturbed for buildings. The automobiles that now flock into the basin courtesy of improved highways have produced significant air pollution. In 1970, a new interstate planning authority, the Tahoe Regional Planning Agency, was created to coordinate the various levels of government in two different states, in order to protect the lake against further deterioration in water and air quality. Its efforts, like those relating to water storage at Tahoe, continue to be controversial, and substantial success is yet to be demonstrated.

The increased population has also intensified pressures for land development. As the region becomes more popular, the very qualities of beauty and isolation that originally attracted visitors are being jeopardized. Sporadic attempts to preserve Lake Tahoe lands in a national park began in the late nineteenth century, and although a forest reserve was established in 1899 in what is now Desolation Wilderness, much of the basin continued to be privately owned. Currently there are three national forests at Tahoe: El Dorado National Forest to the south (including Desolation Wilderness), Lake Tahoe National Forest on the north, and Toiyabe National Forest to the east. Expansion of these areas and purchases of park land by the states and local governments of California and Nevada have enlarged the amount of publicly controlled land in the Tahoe basin to over 70 percent, but much of the shoreline in particular is in private hands.[37] This land has grown ever more valuable, and pressures for its intensive development mount. Yet part of the enduring appeal of Lake Tahoe is its apparent naturalness, which vanishes as condominiums and T-shirt shops multiply.

This inherent contradiction shapes the contemporary debate over human intervention in Tahoe's landscape. In the nineteenth century, human impact on the landscape was sweeping and obvious, as forests were converted to cordwood and the lake was dammed to float the logs downstream. For the most part, especially in the early stages, this human intervention was also supported. William Cullen Bryant, for instance, described his 1872 railroad trip up the Truckee River canyon in approving terms, predictably noting the picturesque cliffs and thundering water, but also "the buzzing saw-mills of an incipient civilization [which] hum with a homelike, New-England sound on its banks."[38] Conquest of nature by civilization, as represented by the sawmills, was for Bryant and many others a token of progress. And progress was the quintessential American value.

The modern Tahoe landscape, too, is heavily affected by human interventions such as automobiles and sewer systems; but contemporary attitudes toward the transformation are more ambivalent. Ski runs and casinos, and the restaurants and hotels they engender, all have their partisans; but wilderness advocates argue that the pollutants they produce endanger the very existence of pristine alpine lakes. In an atmosphere of environmental crisis, human dominion over nature no longer signifies unmitigated progress as it did for Bryant. Progress is still a prevailing social value, but the exact direction in which it lies is no longer clear.

So environmental alteration continues at Tahoe, as it has done since Frémont's "discovery." Now, however, the process is overseen by government authority in order to minimize its impact. The lake level is controlled, logging is severely limited, trout spawning is supervised, and building heights and locations are prescribed, all in the name of protecting Lake Tahoe. The various environmental regulations create an intensively managed landscape that has changed tremendously from the one that John Frémont saw in 1844. Yet the modern changes, unlike their nineteenth-century predecessors, are self-conscious. Increasingly, they are being carefully designed to disguise the extent of their impact. Rather than proclaiming human dominion over nature, current practices seek to minimize perceptible alteration of the region in the name of natural preservation. A historical evolution in the image of Lake Tahoe, the ways that it is perceived, has dictated a different approach to manipulation of its environment in the late twentieth century.

The nature of this shift in image is clear in contemporary accounts of the lake. The earliest nineteenth-century accounts focus on the potential for multifaceted development in the basin. In 1862, the *Sacramento Union* reprinted a proud notice of activity at the lake, including construction of a $500 bridge over the Truckee River, production of 450 tons of hay by six different companies, profitable commercial trout fishing, and remodeling of several local inns.[39] All of these changes clearly symbolized improvement to the writer. They were celebrated as signs of the times, tokens of a bright future when the landscape would be of ever greater use to its new inhabitants. When lumbering began, it, too, was admired as part of the scenery by visitors like Isabella Bird. In 1873, she commented on the logged-over landscape in terms that seemed effortlessly to meld human influences with natural ones. Describing the vast number of pines, she wrote:

> Their stumps and carcasses were everywhere; and smooth "shoots" [chutes] on the sierras marked where they were shot down as "felled timber," to be floated off by the river. To them this wild region owes its scattered population, and the sharp ring of the lumberer's axe mingles with the cries of wild beasts and the roar of mountain torrents.[40]

The modern environmental ethos sharply distinguishes between natural areas and those altered by human interference, but the mid-nineteenth century did not make such a clear distinction. William Cullen Bryant was not alone in finding the hum of Truckee River sawmills comforting. In 1884, a guidebook described the wonders of the drive from Truckee to Tahoe City:

> Then you have the Truckee River with you all the way—that matchless mountain streamlet of pure ice-cold water. Tree, bush, and flower grow and blossom upon either side; and a little bird, with a throat like a thrush, warbles a canticle of exquisite musical modulations, so to speak. But *the most stirring sight of all is the system of logging carried on by the mill companies.*[41]

In this period both natural and manmade attractions were perceived to be scenic. Mountain vistas and lumber mills were jumbled together indiscriminately on the list of sights that tourists were admonished to see in order to have a proper experience of Tahoe.[42]

Although there *were* nineteenth-century voices of environmental caution, they seemed to focus on waste rather than on the wisdom of using the resources. Thus in 1877, Henry R. Mighels warned about the taking of too many fish, lest there be "a complete annihilation of the native mountain trout." Mighels didn't want an end to fishing, however, just a replenishment of trout streams each season.[43] And even John Muir—who in later years became the most renowned voice of the preservation movement and argued strenuously against even the beneficial development of areas like Yosemite and Hetch Hetchy—was relatively mild in his observation of logging at Tahoe: "The destructive action of man in clearing away the forest has not as yet effected any very marked change in general views. . . . But the business is being pushed so fervently from year to year, almost the entire basin must be stripped ere long of one of its most attractive features."[44] Here Muir seems to advocate caution, rather than abandoning logging altogether. He goes on in the same article not to lambaste lumbering, but to explain that winter is the best time to visit the lake because the commotion produced by loggers and frivolous summer tourists alike is quieted then.

For most nineteenth-century Tahoe visitors, natural beauty was entirely consistent with commercial use. Tourists admired the lake's dazzling clarity and sought refreshment in its cooling breezes and inspiration from the surrounding granite peaks. They also, for the most part, esteemed its commercial potential and the fabulous logging operations along its banks. Until the devastation from the latter grew overwhelming in the 1890s, both natural and economic uses of Tahoe were deemed equally desirable. They were commonly juxtaposed by contemporary observers such as Bryant and Bird, or again in this 1877 paean to Tahoe: "Here was the limpid heart of the Sierras; and the wild, the picturesque, and the sublime, all combine to enhance its conceded beauty. California herself, ever alive to her own interests, was also entertaining some very utilitarian views with regard to it."[45] The lake's scenery had a moral and restorative influence on individuals, while its sawmills and resorts were the physical incarnation of progress for the society as a whole. Beauty and utility were not inconsistent.

By the end of the nineteenth century, however, a painful physical lesson was being learned at Lake Tahoe. The earlier ideal of balanced use, of combining individual and social progress at one location, gave way to a new rhetoric of regret, as in a 1903 *Sunset* article:

> The shore of Tahoe was once heavily timbered with magnificent pines, but the giant stumps are now the only evidence of this superb tree growth. The trees were ruthlessly cut years ago and the pity of it is that most of the timber went into the underground workings of the Comstock mines. The second growth of pine and fir serves to save the shores and the mountain sides from bareness, but it is a poor substitute for the primeval forest that would have lent dignity and grandeur to the lake.[46]

Economic exploitation by the lumber companies had jeopardized Tahoe's beauty. Overuse of the environment had led to its deterioration.

More than 60 percent of the land in the Tahoe basin had been logged, and the integrity of the watershed was jeopardized. There were numerous proposals to protect the lake by turning it over to public management. The preservationist Sierra Club began in 1896 to campaign for a national park to be established at Lake Tahoe.[47] The Bliss family offered to turn their extensive Tahoe acreage (now fully logged) over to the federal government in 1900 so that a national park could be created. Others advocated management of Tahoe lands by the University of California, or by the state. Although none of these plans was ultimately successful, the federal government *did* create a Lake Tahoe Forest Reserve southwest of the lake in 1899. This was expanded in 1905, and joined later by other park and forest lands purchased by county, state, and federal governments. Once seen as a natural setting for investment and exploitation, Tahoe in the twentieth century came to be regarded by some groups as endangered.

Simultaneously with this environmental shift from use to protection, the literary depiction of Lake Tahoe also changed. Guidebooks and travelers stopped promiscuously combining natural and manmade attractions. Instead they gave primacy to Tahoe's natural features, proclaiming their enduring beauty despite the pressures of change. A 1911 *Sunset* article reassured its readers that "Tahoe will ever remain the same. No matter how advancing civilization may introduce new inventions and new luxuries, still nature around the Tavern in a thousand centuries will hold out to the wearied dwellers of the sea-level inspiration of life and serenity of soul."[48] Guidebooks were now recommending camping outdoors at Tahoe, active immersion in nature rather than passive viewing from a boat: "One must get out and feel the bigness of it all; climb its mountains, follow its trout streams; ride or walk or push one's way through its leafy coverts. . . ."[49] Tourists were advised to come in the winter season in order to find the "real Tahoe," free from the noise and artifices of the summer tourists.

The more that physical change intruded at Lake Tahoe, the less it was countenanced in the imagery. Twentieth-century visitors still discussed the traditional lake features of color, clarity, beauty of scenery, and opportunities for relaxation, but no longer with their earlier innocence. Now they were mindful also that human activity in the basin had badly polluted the Truckee River with sawdust, and that further development of water storage capacity was threatened. By 1918, one writer was reassuring her readers that the lake was invulnerable, "nature here in all her phases attesting to the power of something before and beyond man's dominion."[50] Yet the record of human intervention at Tahoe actually suggested quite a different lesson. Far from being beyond human dominion, the lake was in fact frighteningly fragile.

Overdevelopment loomed as a danger even in 1915, when George Wharton James observed in *The Lake of the Sky* that part of Tahoe's attractiveness was the relative absence of people. Yet he feared that "as the men of California and Nevada cities find more time for leisure it will not be many years before every available spot will be purchased and summer residences abound. . . ." By 1941 this prediction had apparently come true. Max Miller observed in that year that the area "has been ruined . . . by too much publicity which brings too many people in summer. Most of the shoreline around Tahoe, huge though it is, is privately owned, and built-up, and rented."[51] Lake shore that is built up and rented may bring prosperity to the sellers and owners, but its population endangers the very solitude and beauty that drew people to Tahoe in the first place. With year-round recreation, even the isolation of winter at the lake has now been broken.

For modern residents, the dilemma is a serious one. If Tahoe no longer offers visitors the chance to experience untrammeled nature, or some reasonable facsimile thereof, then all the recreational variety offered by casinos and ski runs may be insufficient to sustain its tourist economy. The modern tourist industry at Lake Tahoe is based not solely on beauty, but on the increasingly rare chance to enjoy nature as well. Accordingly, the landscape is now vigorously managed so as to appear, paradoxically, pristine. Thus architecture at Tahoe is determinedly rustic, with wooden buildings painted in tasteful, unobtrusive colors. Local ordinances dictate that commercial signs be small and subdued. Automobile traffic is officially discouraged in favor of bicycle paths and public transit systems. The Tahoe Regional Planning Agency prohibits development of certain environmentally sensitive lots. In the twentieth century, new prevailing styles of tourism and recreational preferences have combined to create a different landscape ethos at Lake Tahoe. Far from celebrating human dominion over nature, as their nineteenth-century predecessors did, twentieth-century residents of the basin seek to diminish visible signs of their intrusion into the landscape, so that others may continue to enjoy it as a beautiful natural environment.

In 1862, when he first saw Lake Tahoe, Thomas Starr King mused about that beauty. Like many before him and millions since, he found it both stimulating and relaxing: "To a wearied frame and tired mind what refreshment there is in the neighborhood of this lake! The air is singularly searching and strengthening. The noble pines, not obstructed by underbrush, enrich the slightest breeze with aroma and music."[52] Yet he also worried that "Tahoe has been wasted because so few appreciative souls have studied and enjoyed it." No twentieth-century observer of the region would share his worry that the lake was wasted for lack of an audience. For modern lovers of Tahoe, the difficulty is rather how to balance a growing audience with a vulnerable landscape, and somehow preserve at least some semblance of the natural qualities that originally inspired King's glowing tribute.

As the photographic pairs demonstrate, development of Tahoe has involved considerable physical change. The contemporary lake landscape is *not* the same one King would have seen in 1862. It has been substantially modified by human intervention. The character and intent of that intervention, however, cannot be fully comprehended without also understanding the changing assumptions that have informed the process over time. In the twentieth century, nature at Lake Tahoe has become a valuable commodity. It is manipulated and protected in order to look pristine, to conform as closely as possible to the image created and perpetuated by generations of admiring visitors like Thomas Starr King.

Notes

1. The phrase comes from a guidebook by Ben C. Truman, *Tourists' Illustrated Guide to the Celebrated Summer and Winter Resorts of California* (San Francisco: H. S. Crocker & Co., 1884), p. 97.

2. Frémont, John Charles. *The Expeditions of John Charles Frémont*, vol. 1, *Travels from 1838 to 1844*. Edited by Donald Jackson and Mary Lee Spence (Urbana: University of Illinois Press, 1970), p. 635.

3. The Washoe migrations continued well into the twentieth century, despite white intrusion. See Winona James, "An Interview with Winona James, Conducted by T. King," Oral History Project, University of Nevada, Reno, 1984.

4. The best overview of Lake Tahoe's environmental development is Douglas H. Strong, *Tahoe: An Environmental History* (Lincoln: University of Nebraska Press, 1984), on which my summary heavily depends. Unless otherwise noted, information on Tahoe's history comes from Strong's book. Also useful is Edward B. Scott, *The Saga of Lake Tahoe*, 2 vols. (Crystal Bay, Nevada: Sierra-Tahoe Publishing, 1957, 1973).

5. J. Ross Browne, "A Peep at Washoe," in *Crusoe's Island* (New York: Harper & Bros., 1864), p. 355.

6. "Description of Lake Bigler," *Alta California*, 7 July 1859.

7. I am indebted for information on Washoe activities at the lake, and

for the derivation of the name "Tahoe" to Professor Kay Fowler, Department of Anthropology, University of Nevada, Reno. See George and Bliss Hinkle, *Sierra Nevada Lakes* (Reno: University of Nevada Press, 1987, reprint of 1949 edition), pp. 259–69, for an account of the name changes.

8. Samuel G. Houghton, *A Trace of Desert Waters: The Great Basin Story* (Glendale, California: Arthur H. Clark, 1976), p. 56.

9. Mark Twain, *Roughing It* (New York: Holt, Rinehart & Winston, 1963), pp. 121, 120.

10. For a comprehensive history of water issues at Lake Tahoe, see W. Turrentine Jackson and Donald J. Pisani, *Lake Tahoe Water: A Chronicle of Conflict Affecting the Environment, 1865–1939,* Environmental Quality Series No. 5 (February 1972), Institute of Governmental Affairs, University of California, Davis.

11. Charles D. Irons, comp., *W. F. Edwards' Tourists' Guide and Directory of the Truckee Basin* (Truckee: W. F. Edwards, 1883), p. 98.

12. Scott, *Saga,* vol. 1, p. 14. In addition to Strong, *Environmental History,* pp. 23–30, see David F. Myrick, *Railroads of Nevada and Eastern California,* 2 vols. (Berkeley, California: Howell-North Books, 1963) for a detailed account of early Tahoe lumbering efforts, and their connection to the railroads. Also useful is Anne Seagraves, *Tahoe, Lake in the Sky* (Lakeport, California: Wesanne Enterprises, 1986).

13. The Carson and Tahoe Lumber and Fluming Company actually grew out of the partnership of Yerington, Bliss & Co., established two years earlier, in 1871. "The Story of Tahoe," *Tahoe Tattler,* 16 August 1940, p. 2.

14. George B. Sudworth, "Stanislaus and Lake Tahoe Forest Reserves, California, and Adjacent Territory," in United States Geological Survey, *Twenty-First Annual Report (1899–1900),* Part 5, *Forest Reserves* (Washington, D.C.: Government Printing Office, 1900), p. 551.

15. Strong, *Environmental History,* pp. 30–31.

16. Marsden Manson, "Observations on the Denudation of Vegetation—A Suggested Remedy for California," *Sierra Club Bulletin* 2 (June 1899), p. 298.

17. "A Day on Lake Bigler," *Sacramento Union,* 9 September 1862.

18. "Lake Tahoe and Its Surroundings," *Alta California,* 16 September 1864.

19. "Letter from Lake Tahoe," *Alta California,* 21 June 1870.

20. John Codman, *The Round Trip by Way of Panama through California, Oregon, Nevada, Utah, Idaho, and Colorado* (New York: G. P. Putnam's Sons, 1879), p. 163.

21. See Bob Shedd, *Lake Tahoe Historical Sketches* (Stateline, Nevada: Mountain Press, 1977), pp. 11–12, for an atmospheric account of the steamer *Tahoe.*

22. Sallie B. Morgan, *Tahoe: Or Life in California, A Romance* (Atlanta: James P. Harrison & Co., 1881), p. 242.

23. John F. Sears, *Sacred Places: American Tourist Attractions in the Nineteenth Century* (New York: Oxford University Press, 1989), pp. 4–10. Although Sears does not treat Lake Tahoe, his discussion of Niagara Falls, Mammoth Caves, and Yosemite are all suggestive of Tahoe. In regard to the latter he notes the importance of photographs, widely circulated in the form of the popular stereographic views, in establishing Yosemite as an icon, an attraction that had to be visited (pp. 123–29).

24. See Seagraves, *Tahoe,* for a thorough account of Lake Tahoe resorts, including many private summer homes as well as those catering to tourists.

25. George Wharton James, *The Lake of the Sky* (New York: Baker & Taylor, 1915), p. 143.

26. Myrick, *Railroads,* vol. 2, p. 430.

27. Katherine Chandler, "Tavern of the Big Water," *Sunset* 26 (June 1911), 657. Peter J. Schmitt has traced the increasing late-nineteenth-century American fascination with nature, perceived as an antidote to urbanization, in *Back to Nature: The Arcadian Myth in Urban America* (New York: Oxford University Press, 1969).

28. John Muir, "Lake Tahoe in Winter," *San Francisco Bulletin,* 1878, reprinted *Sierra Club Bulletin* 3 (May 1900), 119–26; J. C. Fergusson, ed. *The*

Alta California Pacific Coast and Transcontinental Rail-Road Guide (San Francisco: Fred MacCrellish, 1871), p. 157.

29. "Tahoe is the subject of many summer resort letters; a few people venture to winter there, and find the experience delightful." Charles Howard Shinn, "The California Lakes," *Overland Monthly* 18 (July 1891), 17. The woodcut is reprinted in Scott, *Saga of Lake Tahoe,* vol. 2, p. 4.

30. For the ski trains, see Shedd, *Lake Tahoe Historical Sketches,* p. 7; for skating at Donner, see John Corbett, ed., *The Ponderosa Area* (Sparks: Western Printing and Publishing, 1964), p. 39.

31. For 1932 Olympics, see Corbett, *Ponderosa Area,* pp. 33–34; for Squaw Valley and other details of early winter sport activities, see Strong, *Environmental History,* pp. 44–46.

32. Owen F. McKeon, "The Railroads and Steamers of Lake Tahoe," *Western Railroader* 9 (March 1946), p. 18; A. Allan Stafford, *Touring Tahoe* (Carson City: Stafford's Book Shop, 1936).

33. For a general history of the development of these auto camp resorts, predecessors of modern motels, see Warren James Belasco, *Americans on the Road: From Autocamp to Motel, 1910–1945* (Cambridge, Mass.: M.I.T. Press, 1979). For Camp Richardson, see Scott, *Saga of Lake Tahoe,* vol. 1, p. 174.

34. Bethel Holmes van Tassel, *Wood Chips to Game Chips: Casinos and People at North Lake Tahoe* (Sacramento: Spilman Printing Co., 1985), pp. 50–51.

35. For alcohol availability at Tahoe, see Basil Woon, *Incredible Land: A Jaunty Baedeker to Hollywood and the Great Southwest* (New York: Liveright Publishing Corp., 1933), p. 217.

36. For the casino industry at Tahoe, see W. Jackson Turrentine and Donald J. Pisani, *From Resort Area to Urban Recreation Center: Themes in the Development of Lake Tahoe, 1946–1956,* Environmental Quality Series No. 15 (April 1973), Institute for Governmental Affairs, University of California, Davis, pp. 53–56.

37. Strong, *Environmental History,* pp. 187–96, is an excellent summary of recent planning efforts in the Tahoe area. For public ownership of Tahoe basin lands, see pp. 66–87.

38. "The Plains and the High Sierra," originally published 1872, facsimile reprint from revised 1894 edition of *Picturesque America* (Reno: Camp Nevada, 1979), p. 587

39. "Bigler Lake and Vicinity," *Sacramento Union,* 6 September 1862.

40. Isabella L. Bird, *A Lady's Life in the Rocky Mountains* (Norman: University of Oklahoma Press, 1960), p. 12

41. Ben C. Truman, *Tourists' Illustrated Guide to the Celebrated Summer and Winter Resorts of California* (San Francisco: H. S. Crocker & Co., 1884), p. 106. Emphasis added.

42. See also "A Trip Around Tahoe," 1878, quoted in "The Story of Lake Tahoe," *Tahoe Tattler,* 18 July 1941, p. 2.

43. Henry R. Mighels, *Sage Brush Leaves* (San Francisco: Edward Bosqui, 1879), p. 245. The entry is dated 8 August 1877.

44. Muir, "Lake Tahoe in Winter," p. 123.

45. Rusling, *Great West and the Pacific Coast,* p. 439.

46. George Hamlin Fitch, "Some Glimpses of Lake Tahoe," *Sunset* 11 (June 1903), p. 215.

47. See Donald J. Pisani, "Lost Parkland: Lumbering and Park Proposals in the Tahoe-Truckee Basin," *Journal of Forest History* 21 (January 1977), 4–17, for a summary of various preservation efforts.

48. Chandler, "Tavern of the Big Water," p. 659.

49. James, *Lake of the Sky,* p. xii.

50. Ellen M. Del Port, "A Tahoe Serenade," *Overland Monthly* 71, 2nd series (January 1918), p. 20.

51. James, *Lake of the Sky,* p. 254; Max Miller, *Reno* (New York: Dodd, Mead, 1941), pp. 81–82.

52. Thomas Starr King, "Living Water from Lake Tahoe," reproduced in James, *Lake of the Sky,* pp. 367, 371.

Historical and Contemporary Photographs

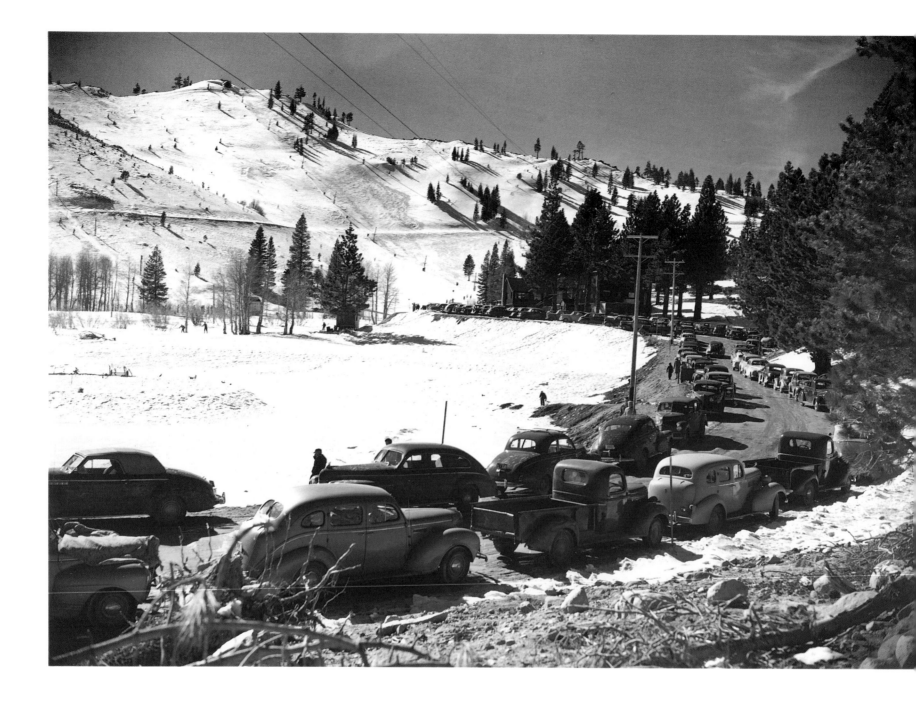

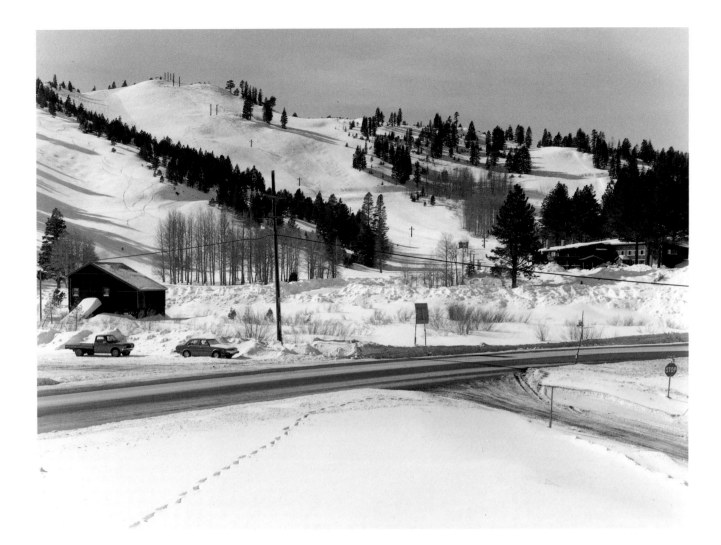

Sky Tavern. The growing popularity of snow skiing has transformed Lake Tahoe into a year-round community from its nineteenth-century status as a summer resort. Sky Tavern is located on the eastern slope of the Sierra Nevada at the junction of Nevada State Route 431 and the old Mount Rose Highway. An early and popular public ski area, it was purchased in the late 1960s for the exclusive use of the Reno Junior Ski Program. At the time, this stipulation met a special need, as children's ski programs were not common at commercial ski areas. Signs in the modern area, on the right, proclaim, "No Sliding, Keep Out, No Parking."

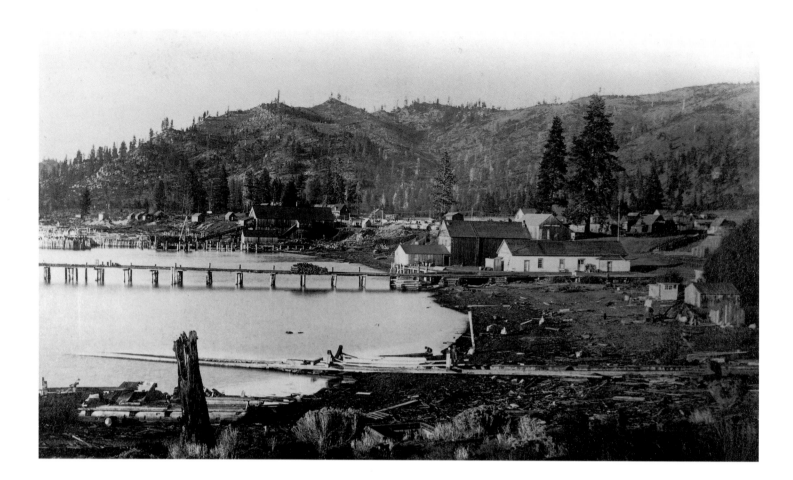

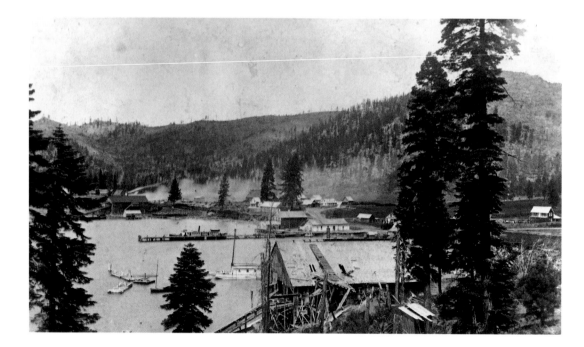

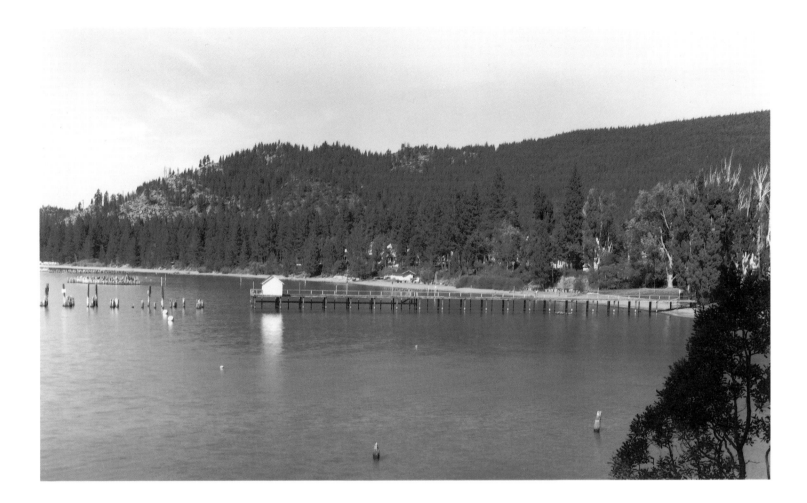

Glenbrook, Nevada. The effects of lumbering were dramatically visible in the 1880s, when the historical photographs on the left were taken. Note the presence of the steamer along the wharf in the bottom left image. Debris from the logging and milling activity created an artificial shoreline at Glenbrook Bay, as tons of sawdust were deposited along the lakeshore. Clear-cutting of trees on mountain slopes accelerated water runoff into the lake. The photograph at top left suggests the truth of one story, that after the Glenbrook area was logged, "only eleven trees were standing as far as the eye could see."

The modern shoreline of Lake Tahoe is also an artificial creation, made possible by the new dam at the outlet to the Truckee River. The dam was completed in 1913, to store water in the lake for downstream users. The maximum storage allowed raised the lake level six feet beyond its "natural" outlet of 6,223 feet above sea level. Seasonal variation in lake level occurred even before water began to be stored there, however, owing to natural cycles of drought affecting the mountain streams that drain into Tahoe.

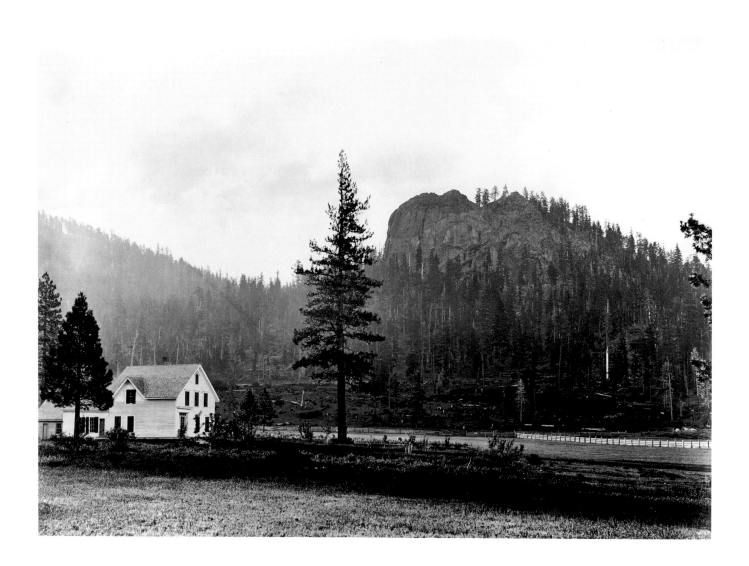

Shakespeare Rock is the prominent landmark at Glenbrook. The name derives from the light marking on the rock that resembles a profile of Shakespeare. It was first noticed by Rev. Mrs. J. A. Benton in 1862 and became a picturesque tourist attraction for nineteenth-century visitors, who speculated on the "divine plan" that had put it there.

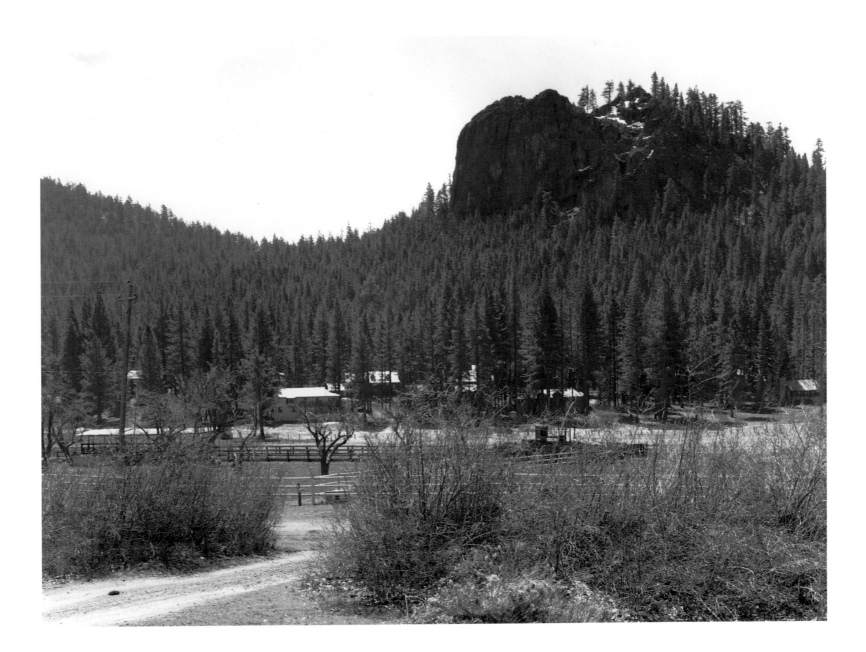

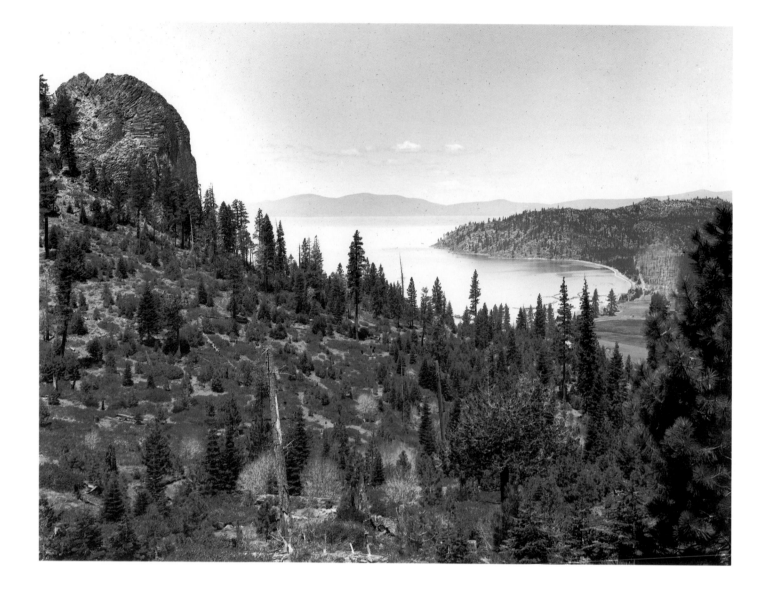

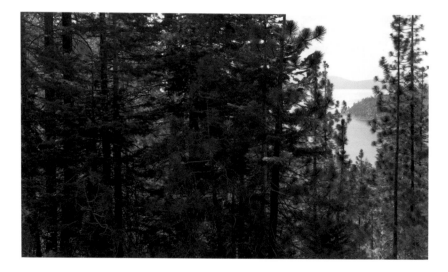

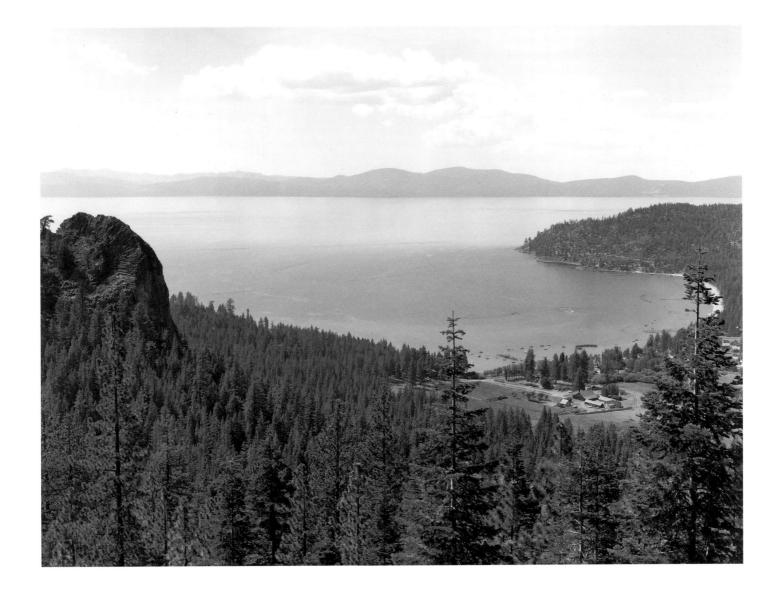

Glenbrook Bay. The historical view at top left is a typical "best general view" of Glenbrook Bay, on the east side of the lake. In the nineteenth century, *best general view* was a term used by photographers to describe the preferred way to record a view of the landscape. By repeating the same view, photographers established a conventional way of seeing certain landmarks.

Because of extensive twentieth-century reforestation, the "best general view" of Glenbrook has changed. The historical vantage point, rephotographed at bottom left, is now almost totally obstructed; only a section of the horizon remains visible. The modern photograph was taken from a point farther up the mountainside, in order to reveal the bay beyond the trees. No longer an industrial center, modern Glenbrook is an exclusive residential community and resort.

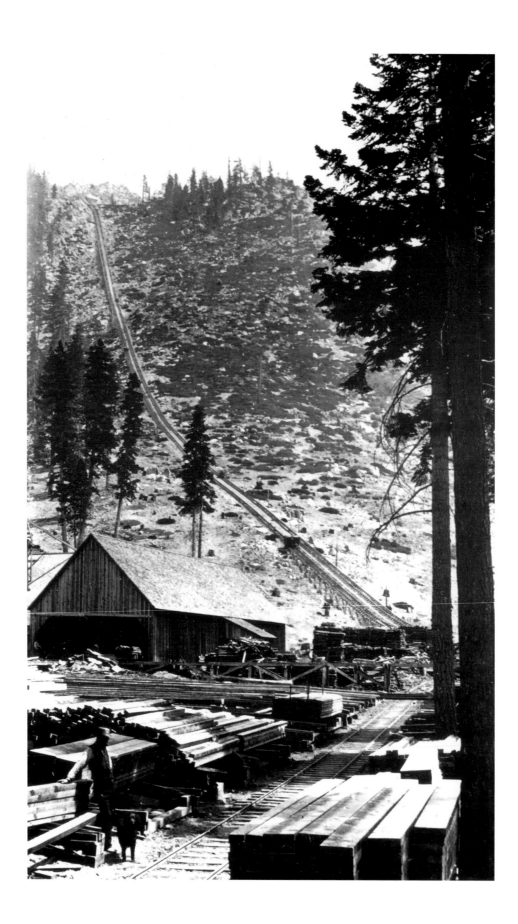

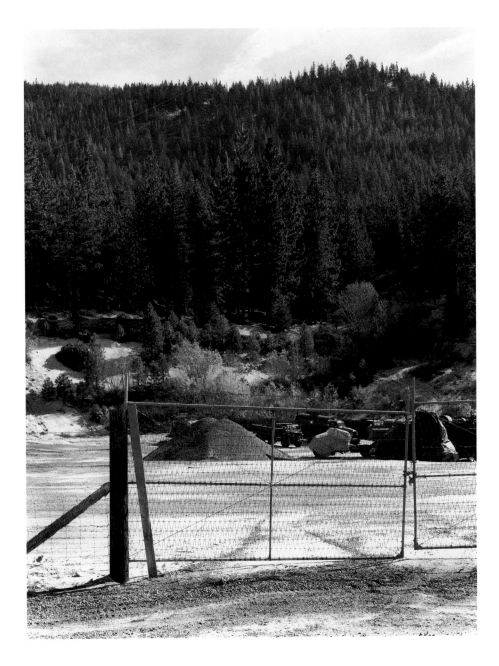

Incline Village, Nevada. The impact of Tahoe lumbering is evident in this 1882 view, on the left, of the famous cable tramway owned by the Sierra Nevada Wood and Lumber Company. Completed in 1880, the incline took lumber from the mill area in the foreground to a flume at the summit, where it made the downhill trip on its way to the Virginia City mines. This site is now on the property of the Ponderosa Ranch, a theme park opened in 1967 and based on *Bonanza*, the popular western television series from the 1960s and 1970s. *Bonanza* was filmed here, and the original flume location has now become a storage lot for maintenance equipment for the Ponderosa Ranch.

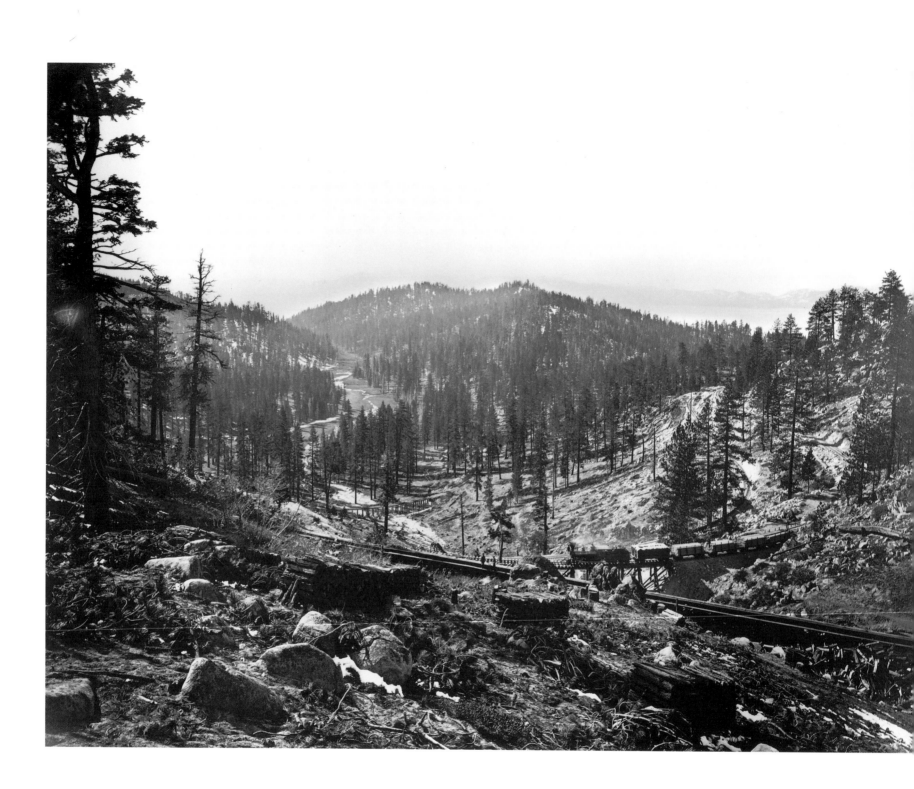

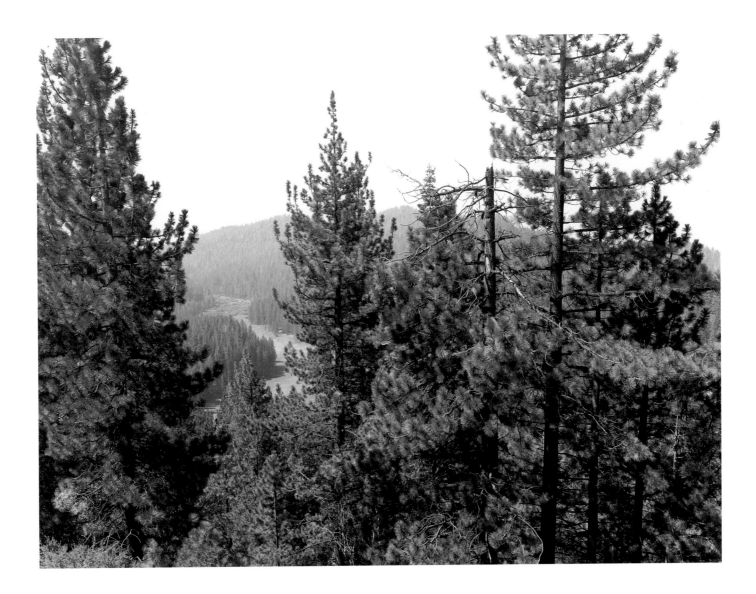

Slaughterhouse Canyon, above Glenbrook. Carleton E. Watkins, *The Z Railroad from Glenbrook to Summit*, c. 1876. The nineteenth-century view of the Carson and Tahoe Lumber and Fluming Company's operation, on the left, depicts the narrow-gauge railroad which hauled logs and lumber products from the mills at Glenbrook to the summit station at Spooner (see next pair). Active logging is clearly visible in the foreground, where felled logs are neatly stacked, and two men are posed near the flume. The debris from logging, in the form of stumps and useless "slash," or small branches, is also evident.

The original vantage point, on what is now State Highway 28, is entirely obscured by trees. The rephotograph was taken from a point farther south in order to provide a modern view of Slaughterhouse Canyon. In the historical photograph, some haze from the mills at Glenbrook is visible. The more extensive haze in the rephotograph resulted from widespread forest fires that were burning in the northern Sierra Nevada.

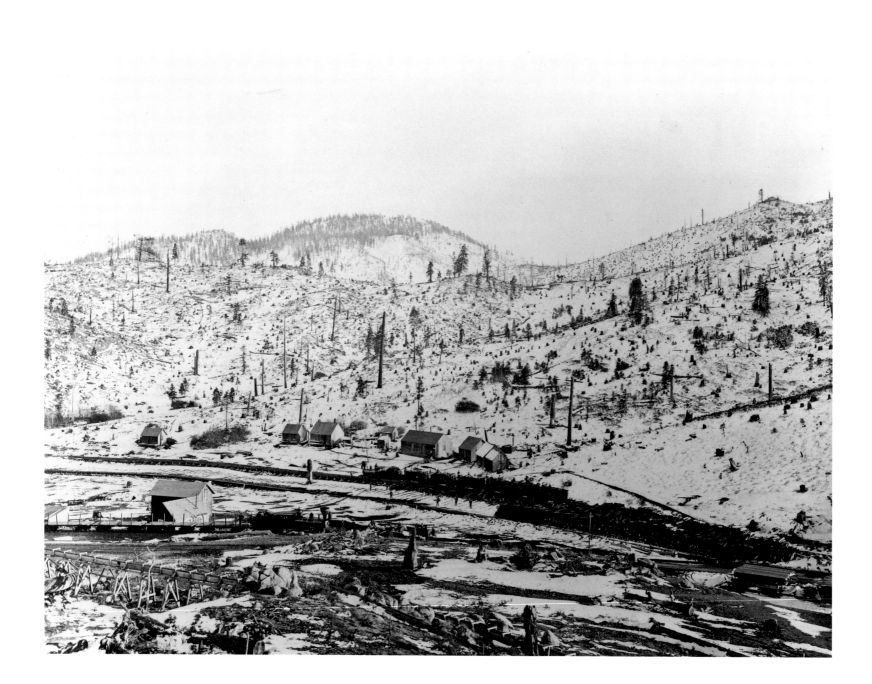

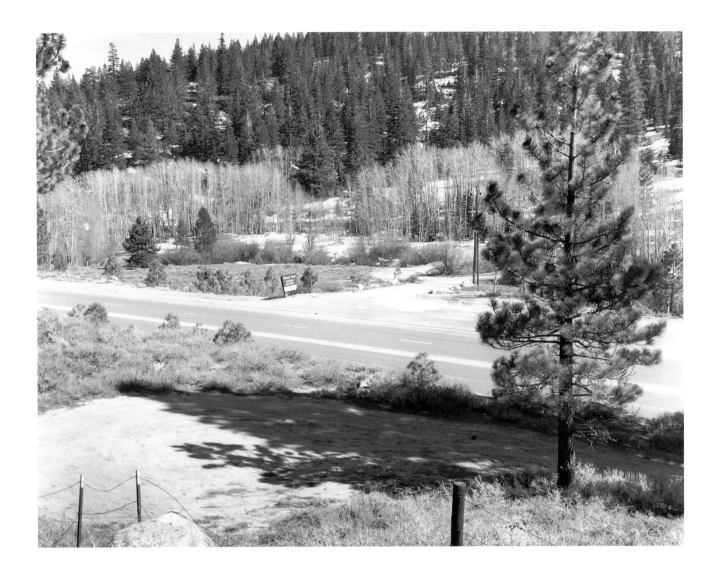

Spooner Summit. Carleton E. Watkins, *Junction of the Virginia and Truckee Railroad at Summit Wood Branch*, 1876. This pair spans more than a century, revealing the full extent of the transformation from the nineteenth-century industrial landscape to an ostensibly "natural" modern Tahoe. The historical photograph at left is a view toward the southeast. It depicts the summit camp of the Carson and Tahoe Lumber and Fluming Company. At this point wood was transferred from the narrow-gauge railroad that brought it up from the lakeside mills at Glenbrook to the flume that would float it down the eastern slope of the mountains to Carson City. Flumes are clearly visible in the left foreground. Loaded cars of cordwood and engines are on the sidings in front of the summit camp buildings. All of the surrounding land has been clear-cut.

Spooner Station was defunct by the turn of the century, when logging at Tahoe declined. The railroad was removed and relocated to Tahoe City. In the modern photograph, on the right, the same area has been designated by the U.S. Forest Service as a picnic and rest area, a place to enjoy the ambience of Tahoe. Second-growth forest, interspersed with aspen, gives little indication of the intensive activity that once took place there. The area is still a major transportation route, however, and Highway 50 is clearly visible.

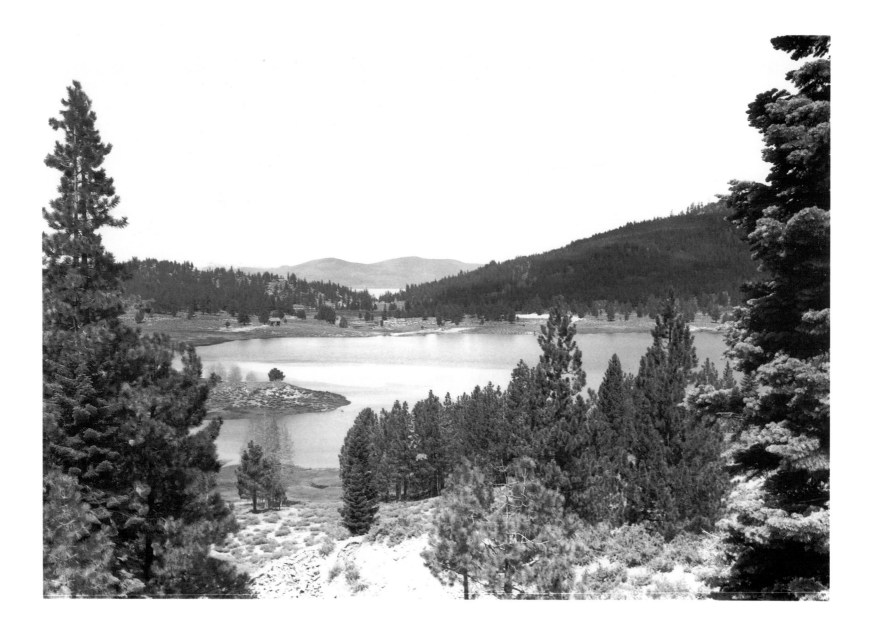

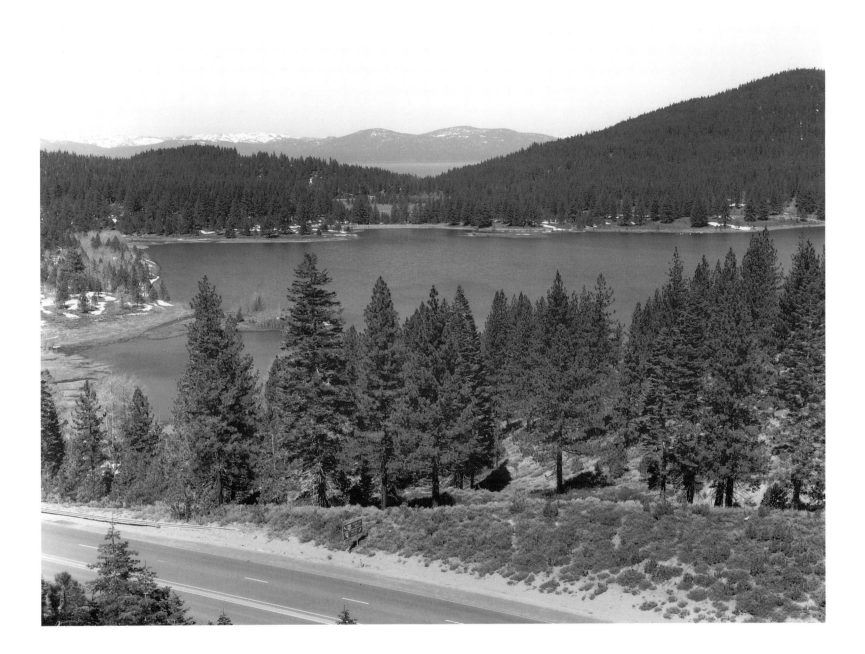

Spooner Lake. This view graphically demonstrates the dynamic character of landscape in the Tahoe basin. Because of regrowth of trees since the height of the timber boom in the 1890s, the original vantage point of the historical photograph at left is no longer available. The contemporary view was taken from a vantage point across the highway and up a steep cliff face. It shows the dam at the far end of the lake, which was originally built to provide water for agricultural irrigation, but is now maintained by the Nevada Department of Fish and Game.

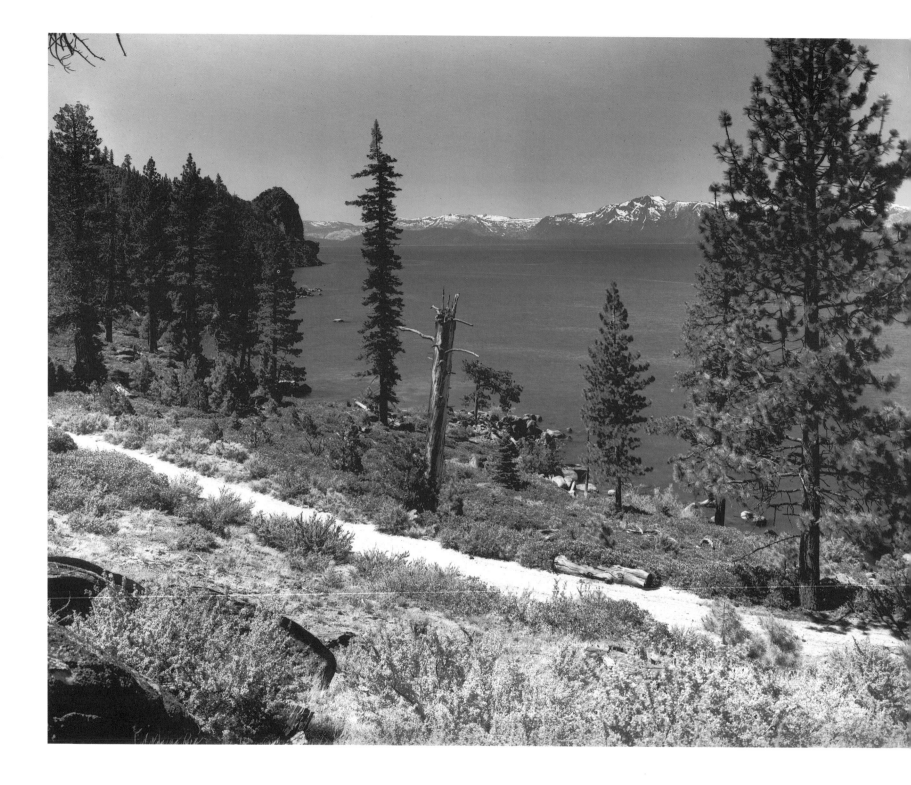

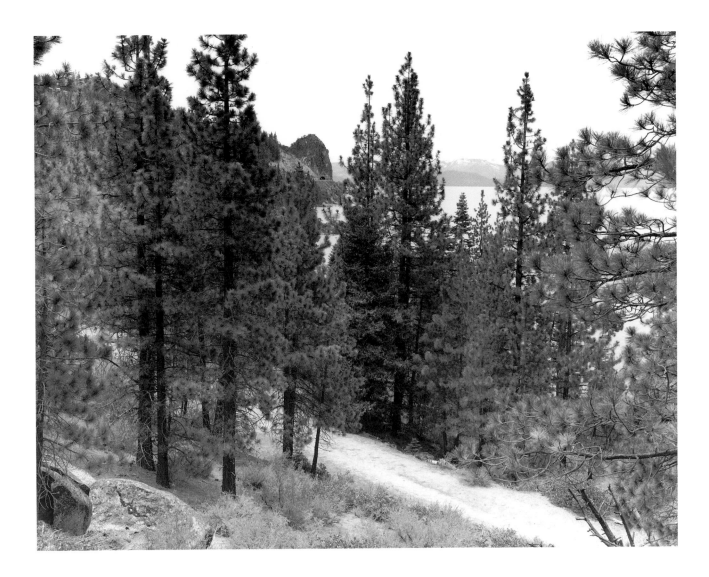

Cave Rock. One of the major landmarks at Lake Tahoe, this site was considered sacred by the Washoe. In the nineteenth century, it became the subject of romantic legends invented specifically for tourists. In keeping with this romanticization is the identification of the "Lady of the Lake," a woman's profile visible on the north side of Cave Rock, when seen from the water. This photographic pair, looking south, was taken from the Logan Shoals area. For the modern shot above, the tripod was suspended in air by a large manzanita bush, the only position providing a view comparable to the historical photograph.

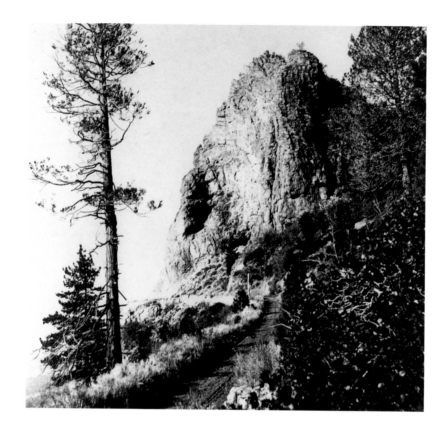

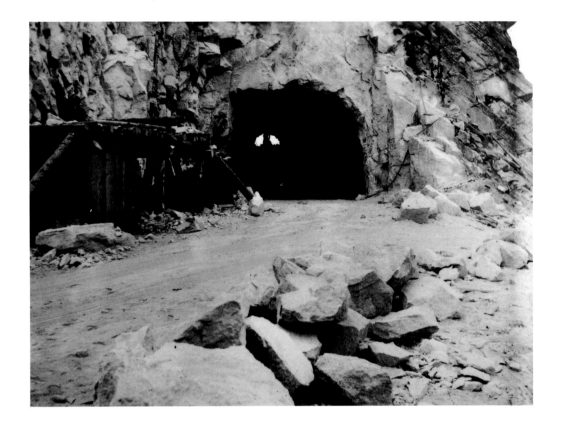

Cave Rock was always an important navigation point for lake travelers, because it was visible from many points. It was a major obstacle to travel *around* the lake, however. Early travelers followed a Washoe trail that went up and around the hill. The 1862 toll road to Carson City circled to the west of the rock on a 100-foot trestle bridge complete with hand-chiseled stone buttresses. The original cave that gave the site its name is clearly visible in the historical image at the left. It was destroyed when tunnels were blasted for the present roadway, Highway 50.

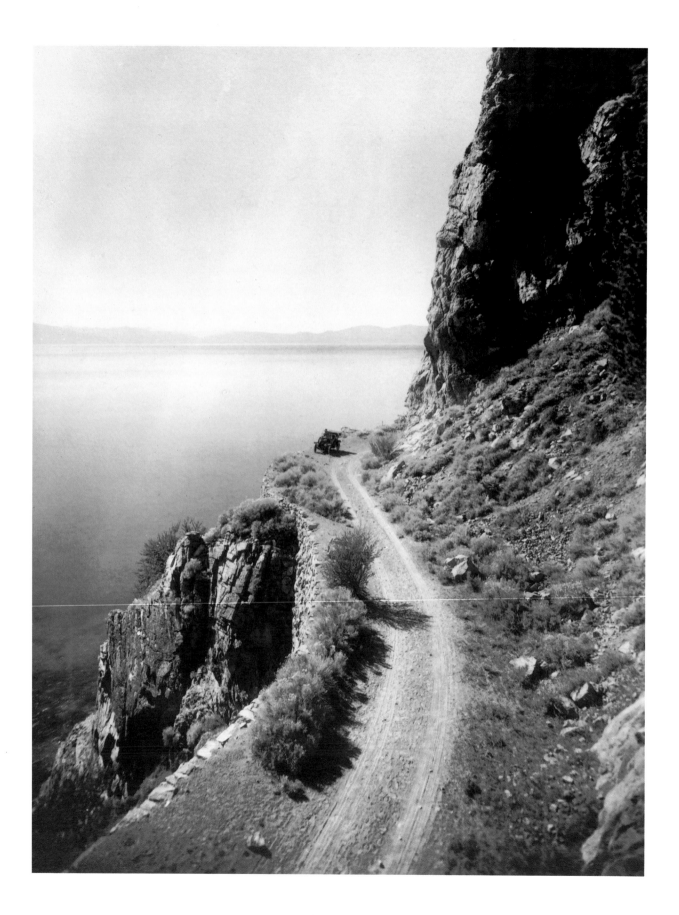

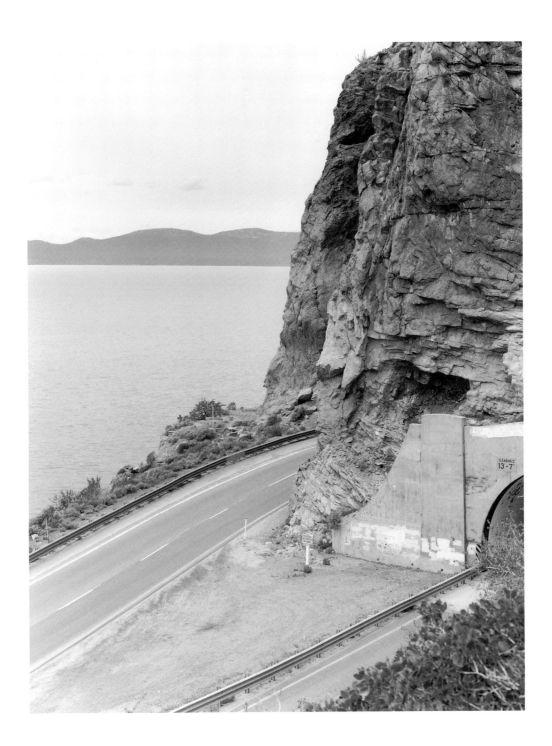

The historical photograph (left) shows the old roadway around Cave Rock. The modern roadway was constructed in two stages. The first tunnel (presently westbound Highway 50) was constructed in 1931. Expansion in 1957 created the second tunnel, visible on the right of the contemporary image.

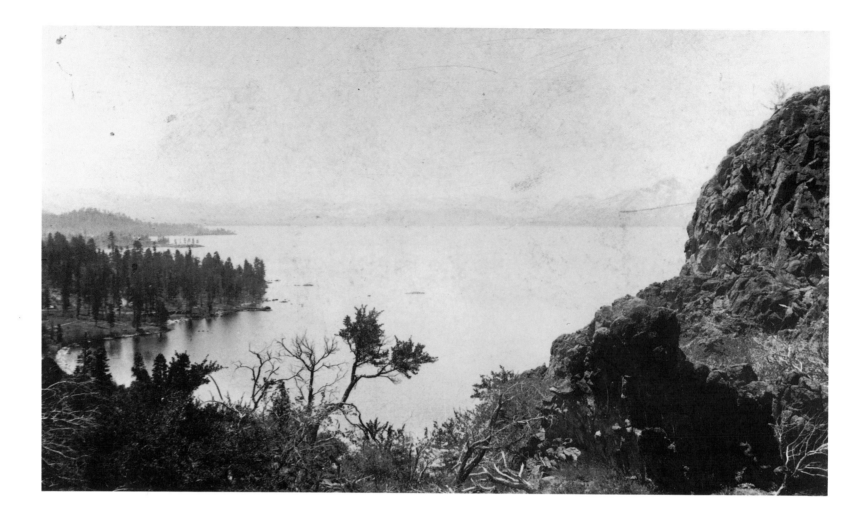

Because the landscape below Cave Rock was only minimally developed when R. J. Waters made the historical image (above), he could not have anticipated the growth hinted at in modern rephotograph at top right. A Nevada state park was created at the site in the late 1960s. The boat launch located there provides public access to some of the renowned outdoor recreational attractions of Tahoe, which is now more frequently experienced from the road than from the surface of the water. The second contemporary image, at bottom right, reveals the full extent of modern commercial development along the road below Cave Rock.

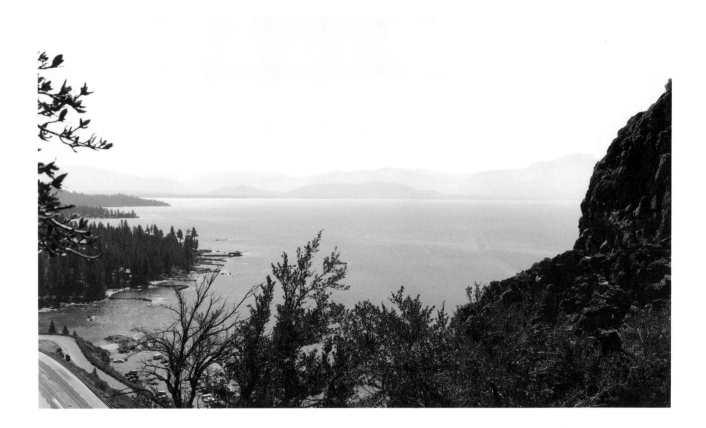

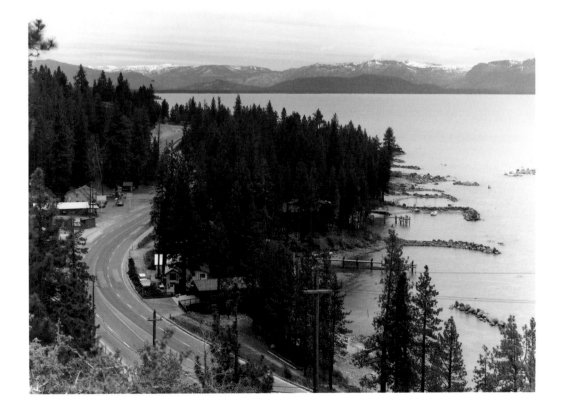

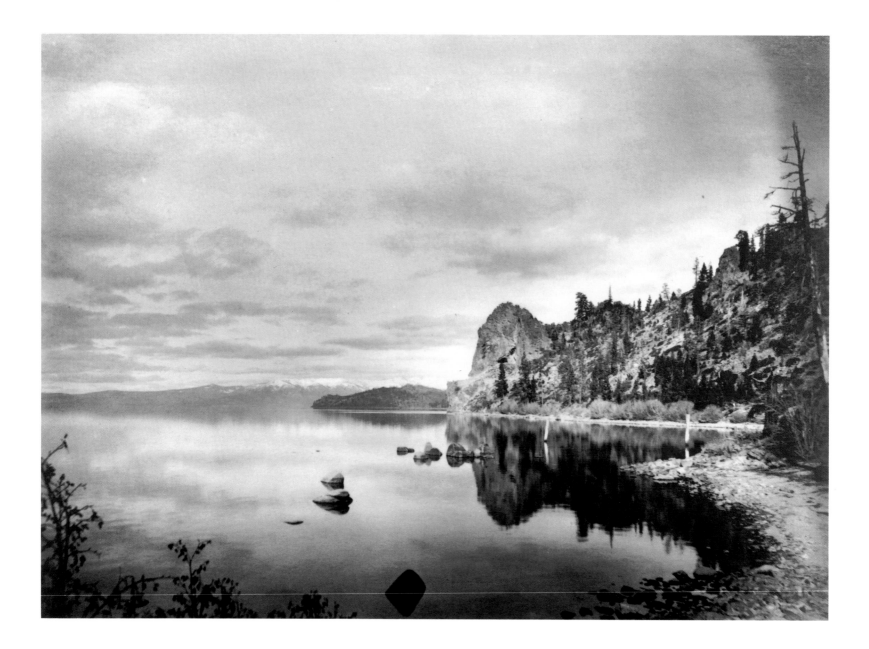

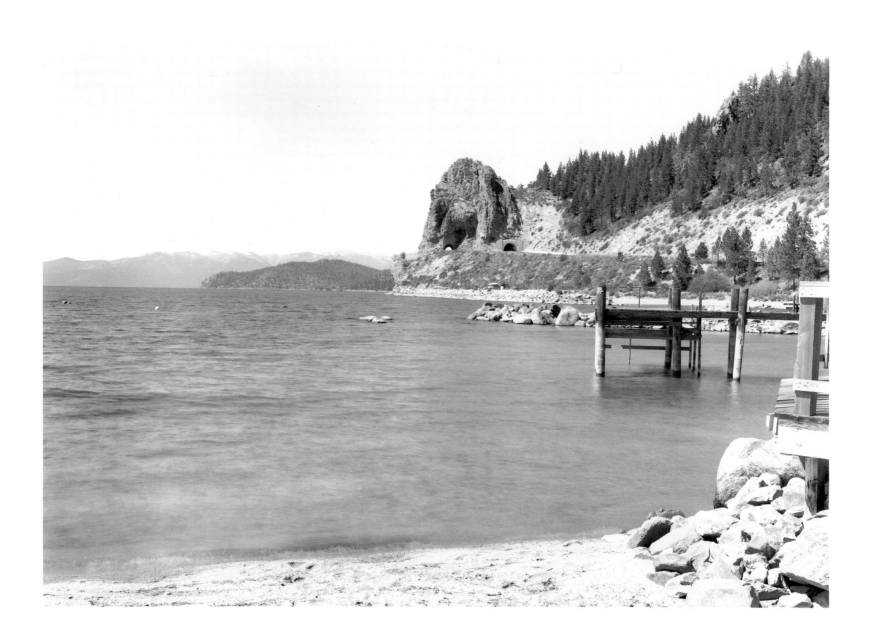

This view is looking north at Cave Rock and its two modern roadway tunnels. Note the second-growth forest visible on the slope above the rock and the marked impact of the road on the landscape. Modern highways that can be kept open in the winter are integral to Tahoe's emergence as a year-round resort.

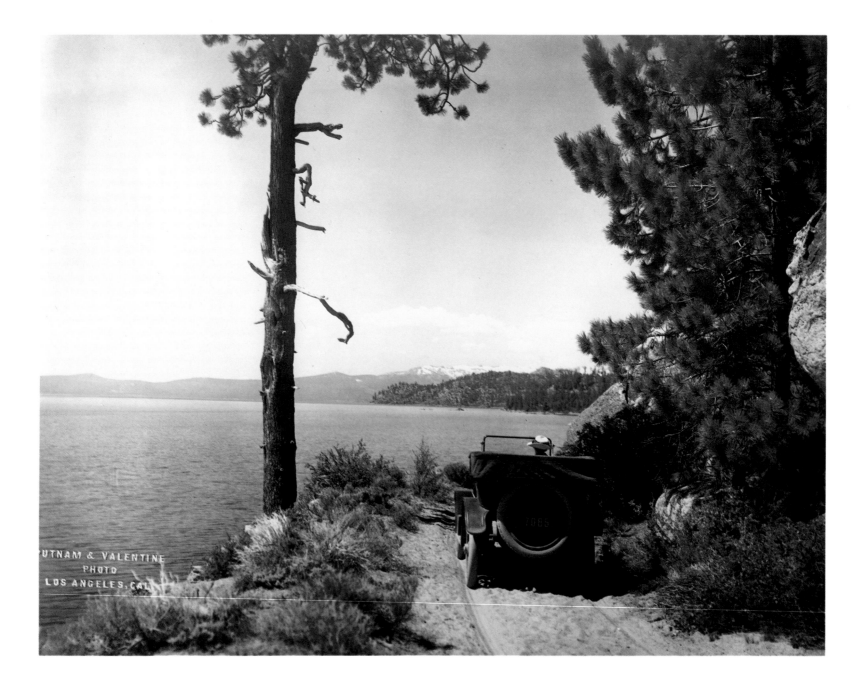

PUTNAM & VALENTINE
PHOTO
LOS ANGELES, CAL.

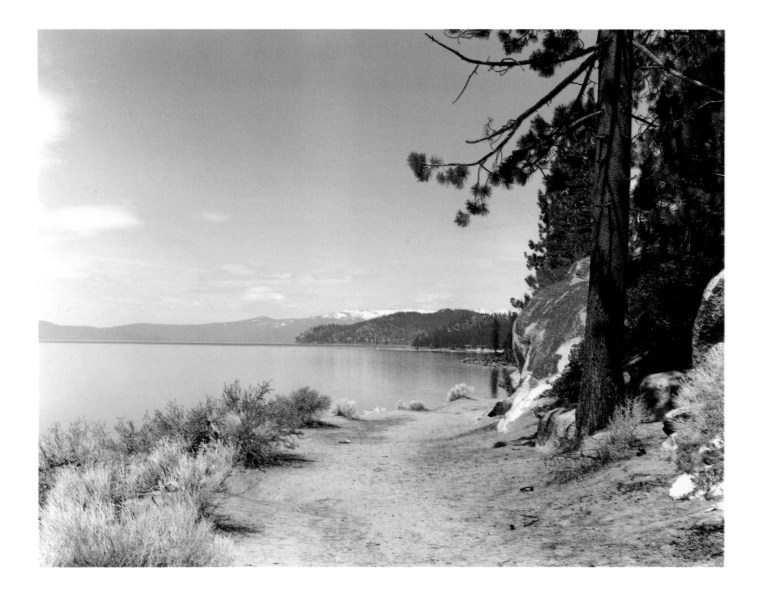

This car and woman (left) appear in a series of documentary photographs taken around Lake Tahoe by C. O. Valentine early in the twentieth century. It was unusual for operators, as photographers were called in the nineteenth century, purposely to record the backs of people. In the historical photograph, which was taken in July 1908, the personality of the woman clearly was not intended to be the subject of the photograph. Her presence was useful to indicate scale, emphasizing the documentary nature of the photograph. Although the road appears quite rustic in the modern rephotograph and is no longer in use, expensive vacation homes (cabins) are now located at its end, just behind the vantage point. Deadman Point is visible in this view to the north.

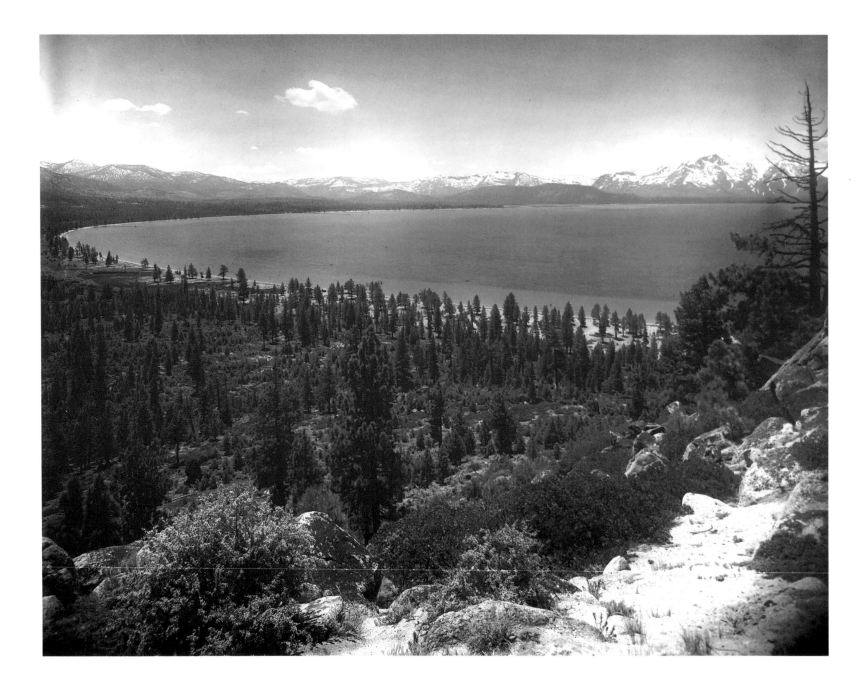

The historical "best general view" of the south shore of Lake Tahoe, above, predates the extensive modern development at Stateline. The Nevada casinos have created a new skyline, and consequently established a different "best general view," top right. This new view nicely juxtaposes two major attractions of the modern tourist industry at Tahoe: casinos and ski resorts. The clear-cut ski runs at the Heavenly Valley Ski Resort, which was founded in 1956, are visible on the mountains just to the right of the casinos. The more precise rephotograph at bottom right does not reveal the extent of landscape change at the south shore of Lake Tahoe.

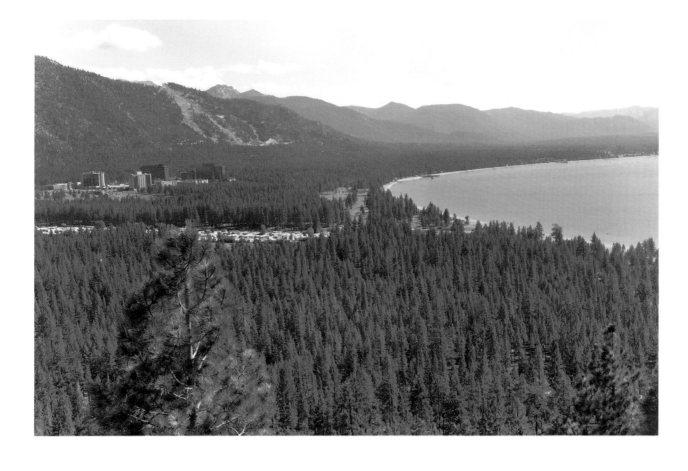

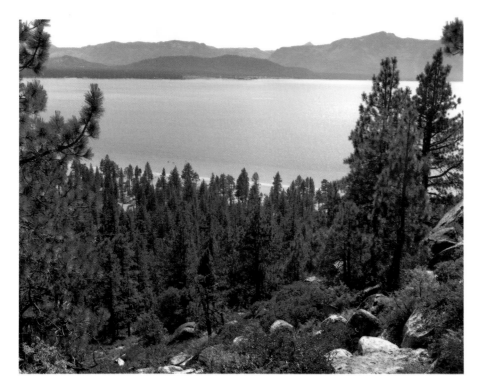

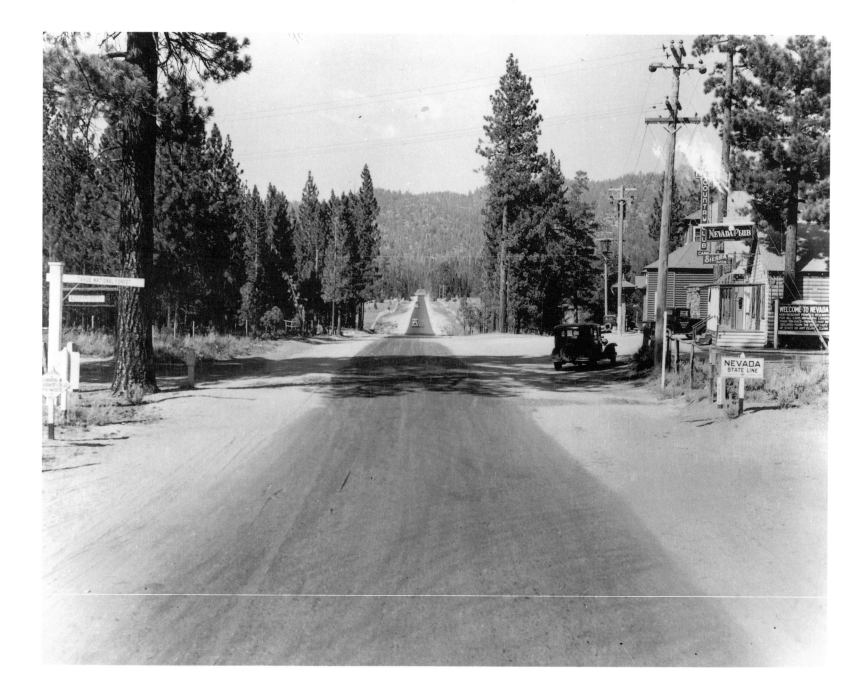

Stateline, Nevada. This pair provides striking testimony to the impact of legalized gambling on the Tahoe landscape. The Nevada Club was a renowned gambling club in the 1920s, but it was not a year-round operation, and the community at the state line was small. Nevada legalized gambling in 1931, and improved winter transportation into the basin after World War II had obvious consequences. The settlement at the lake's south shore, which includes South Lake Tahoe, California, and adjoining Stateline, is presently the largest community at Tahoe. In the words of environmental historians W. Turrentine Jackson and Donald J. Pisani,

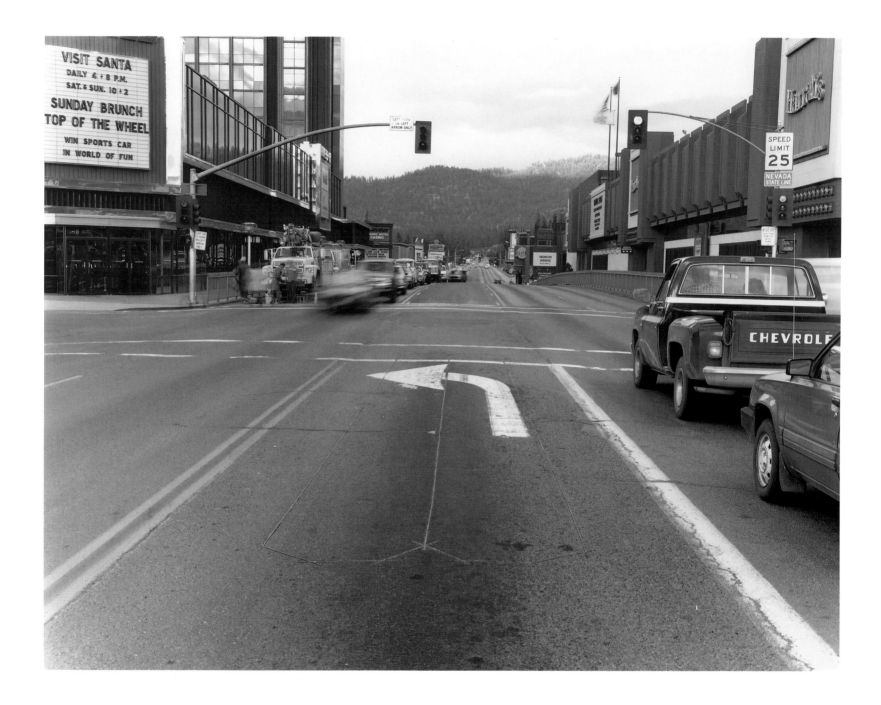

the casinos at Tahoe are a "preeminent symbol of the selling of the environment." Harvey's Wagon Wheel Hotel and Casino, on the left in the modern photograph, and Harrah's Tahoe on the right are both high-rise hotels as well as casinos.

(Turrentine and Pisani, *From Resort Area to Urban Recreation Center: Themes in the Development of Lake Tahoe, 1946–1956*, Environmental Quality Series No. 15 [April 1973], Institute of Governmental Affairs, University of California, Davis, p. 56.)

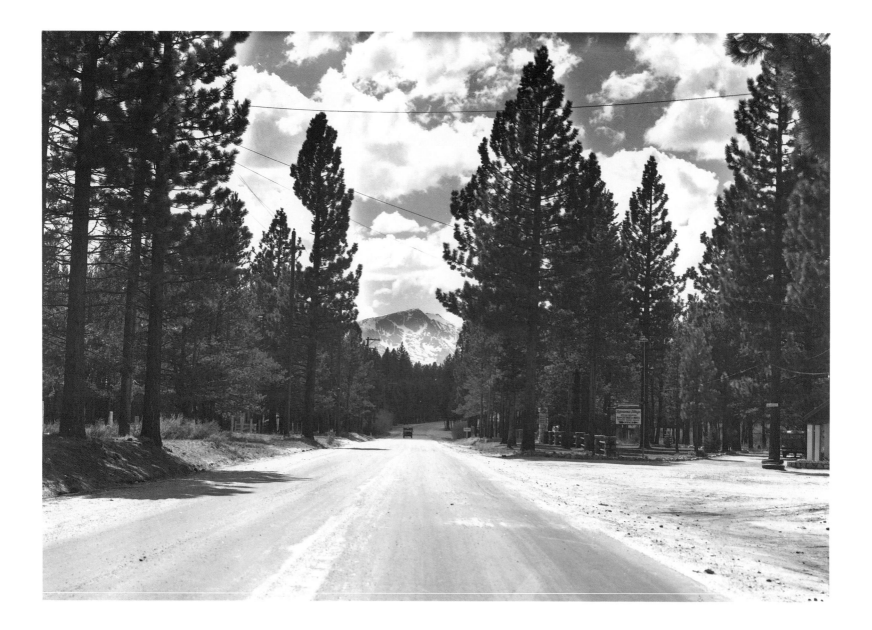

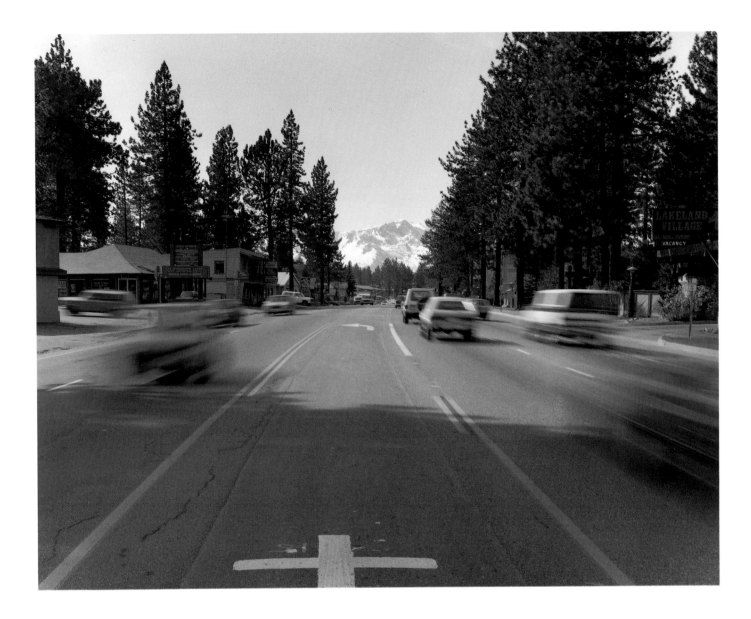

Lakeland Village, South Lake Tahoe. This view is from Highway 50 looking south at Mt. Tallac. Lakeland Village, recorded in both views, was one of the new camp resorts that catered to automobile tourists.

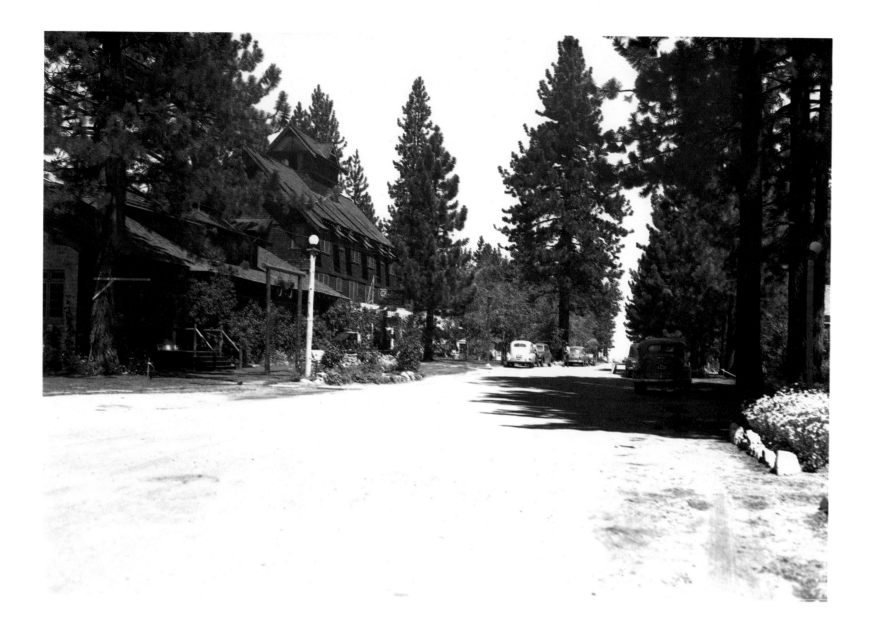

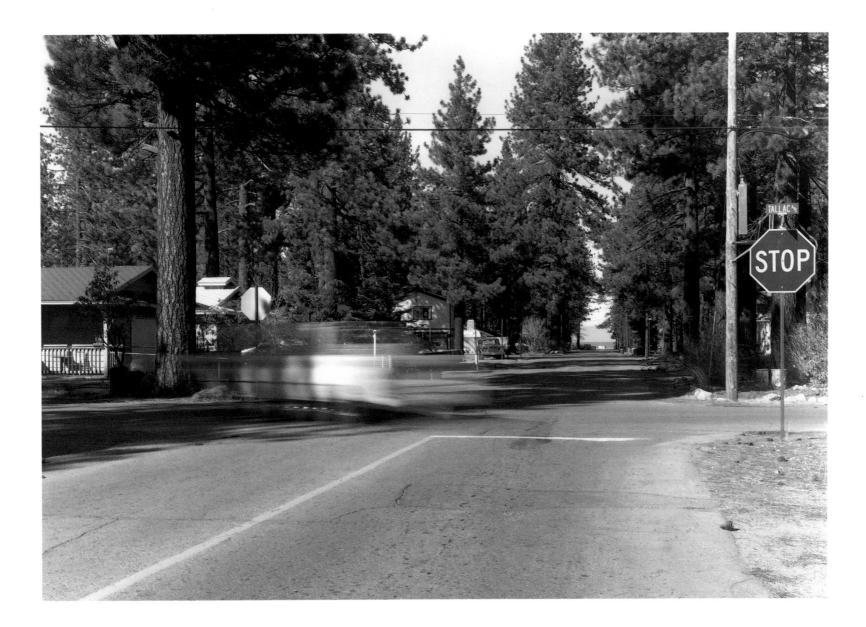

South Lake Tahoe, California. Passing traffic often obscures many views of Lake Tahoe, and this contemporary photograph is no exception. Landscape is not a static entity, but a dynamic fusion of social, political, economic, and environmental forces, which alters greatly over time. Frank Globin purchased the Al Tahoe Inn at this site and opened the Al Globin resort in 1924. In 1940 he expanded, built a new hotel complete with service station, and began to promote Tahoe as a year-round resort. Although it burned down in the 1950s, Globin's was sufficiently popular that it is still one of the sites on a self-guided historic tour of South Lake Tahoe. The leisure activities of visitors over many decades have similarly defined many other significant Tahoe places.

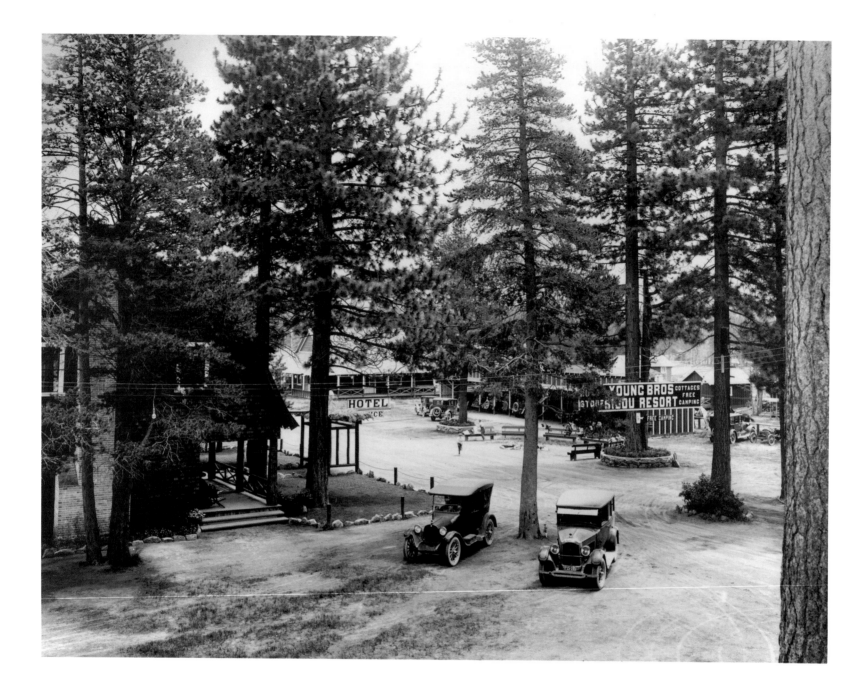

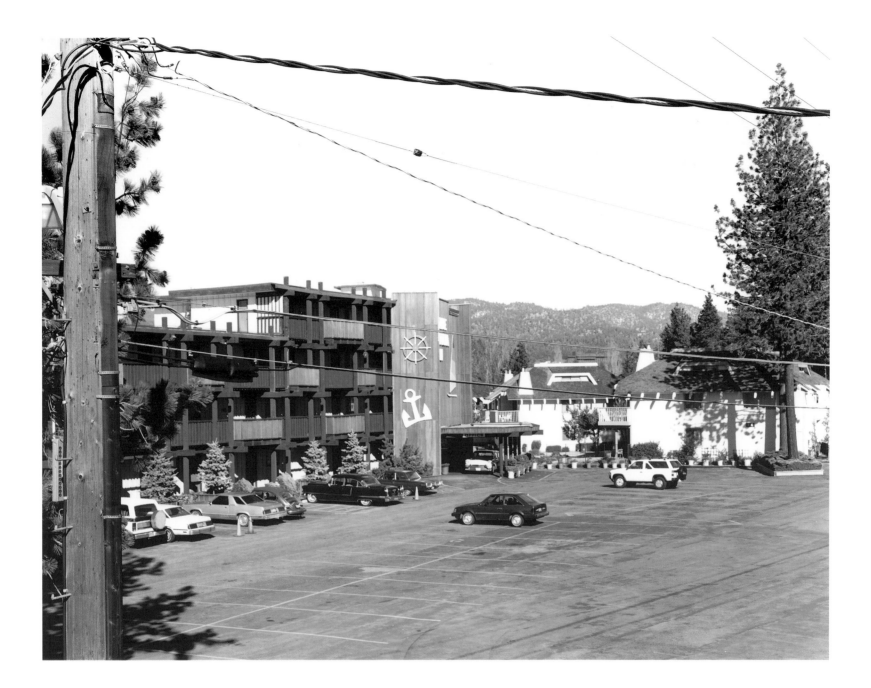

South Lake Tahoe. The Young Brothers Bijou Resort, built early in the twentieth century, is now the site of the Tahoe Marina Inn. The original road artery along Lake Tahoe went through the Bijou Resort. Highway 50, the current artery, is now a few blocks to the east. Note the protective curbing around the trees in the historical view, and how that motif has been preserved in the contemporary location. A denser population has brought more automobiles, however, and there are more parking spaces and fewer trees in the modern photograph.

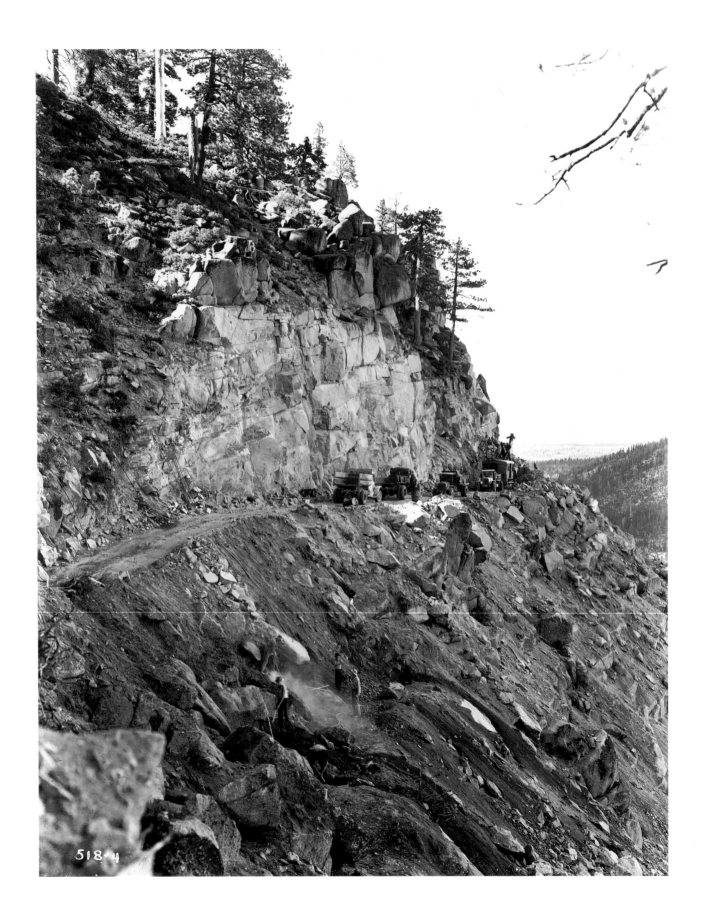

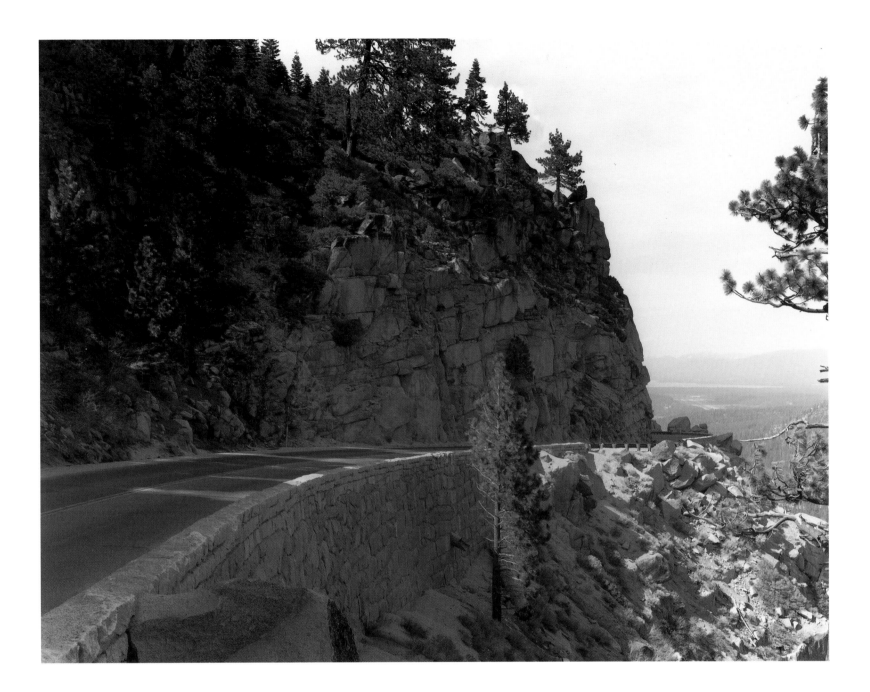

Echo Summit. Construction of the road over Meyers Grade at Echo Summit was photographed in July 1938. Historically, this route was a major thoroughfare from Sacramento and Placerville, California, to Lake Tahoe and Carson City, Nevada. It was designated a state wagon route by California in 1895, and the 1930s improvement was designed to make it more convenient for increasing automobile traffic.

Heather Lake, Desolation Wilderness. The historical photograph (top right) was made with a circuit camera. A Widelux 35mm camera was used to make the rephotograph. The contemporary view was made in October, when the weather was stormy, windy, and rainy. Duplicating some of the hardships of the nineteenth-century photographers, a wait of over two hours was necessary before there was sufficient light to make the modern photograph.

The modern Desolation Wilderness grew from the 1899 Lake Tahoe Forest Reserve, which was established in response to the growing perception that lumbering at Tahoe was destroying the landscape. Although there were numerous proposals to establish a national park at Lake Tahoe, they were defeated. One notable attempt, in 1900, would have turned over to the federal government much of the extensive Tahoe acreage owned by the Carson and Tahoe Lumber and Fluming Company. Because the company would have received other federal lands in exchange for its logged-over land around the lake, however, there was considerable public opposition to the proposal. Some people claimed that the timber company was swindling the public by attempting to trade its bad land for good.

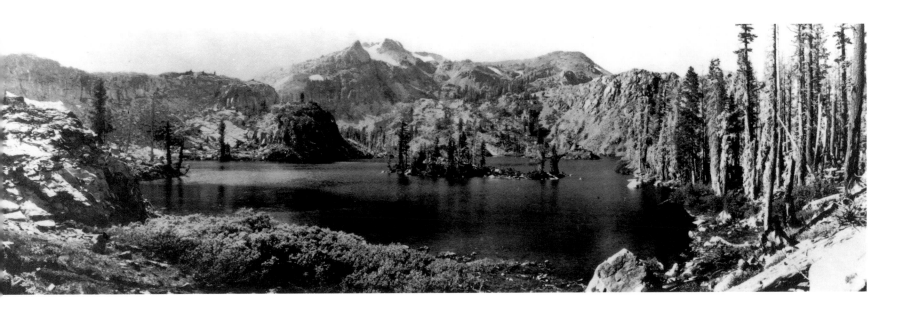

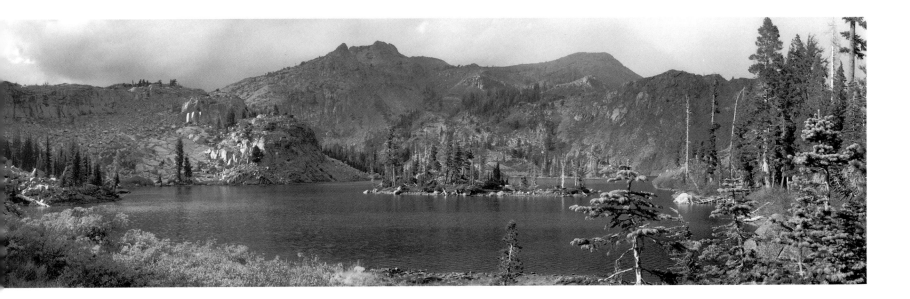

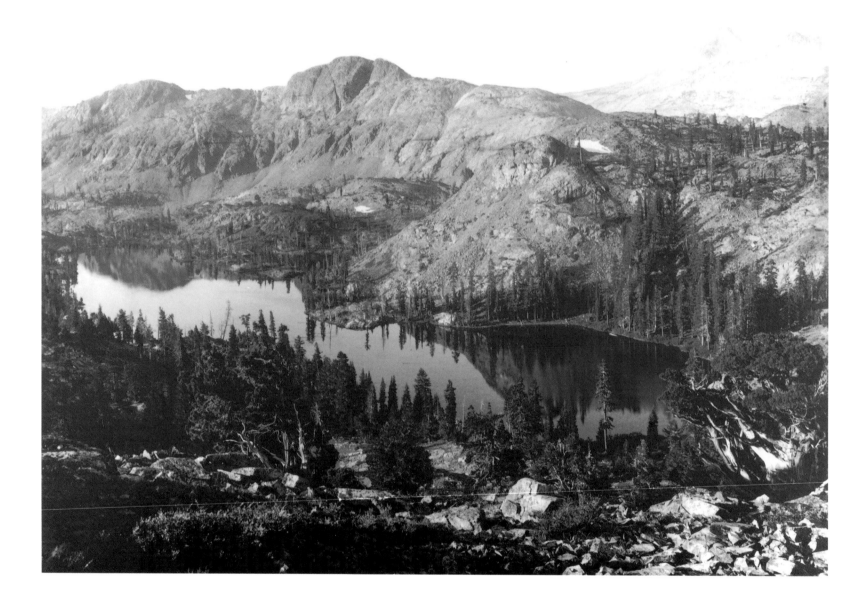

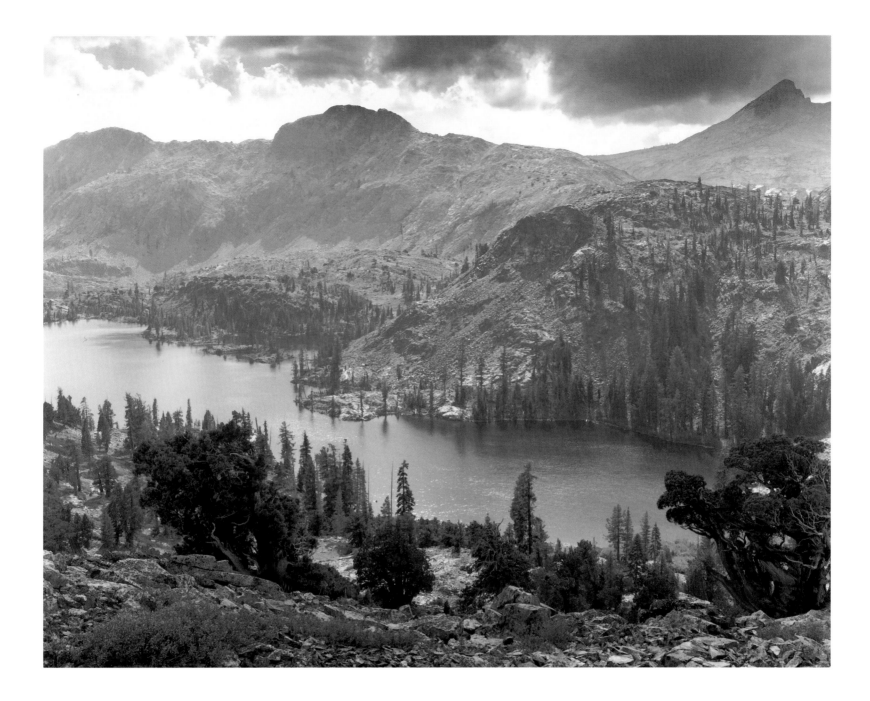

Susie Lake, Desolation Wilderness.

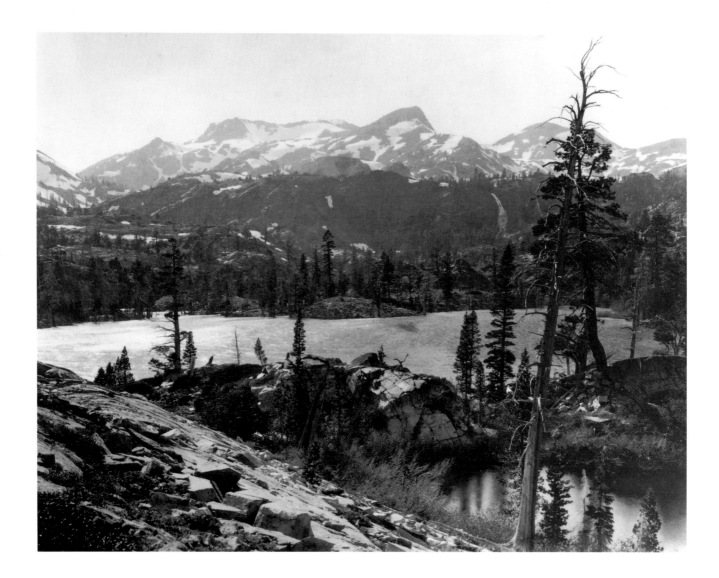

Grass Lake, Desolation Wilderness. Rephotography is not always an exact science.
The photographs were taken from the same vantage point, but at different seasons. The
historical image above, with considerable snow and a waterfall visible on the side of the
mountain, is a spring view. The modern image was taken in the fall, when the snow had
melted and there was no runoff for the waterfall.

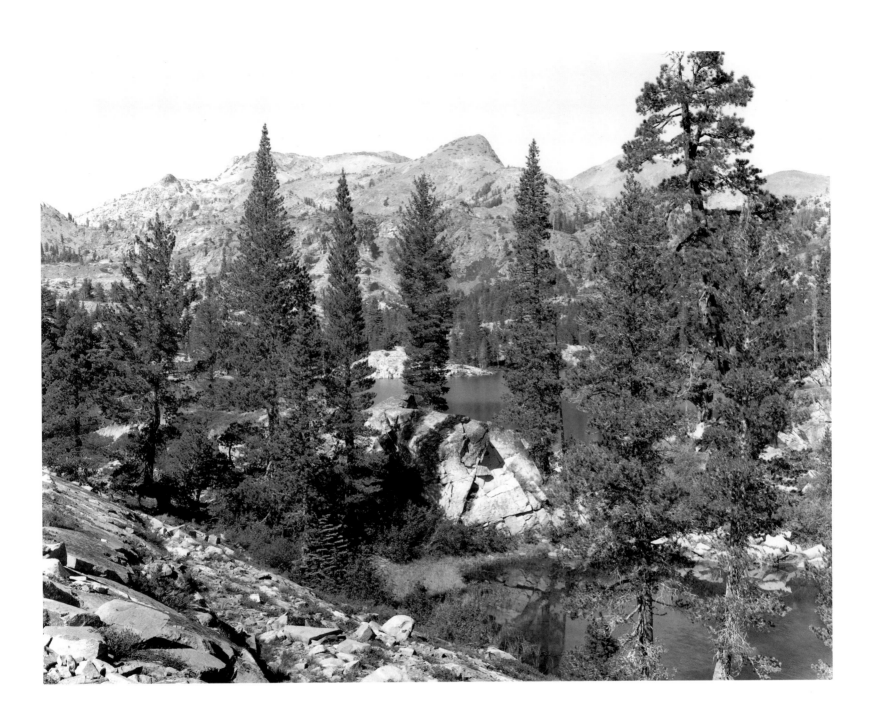

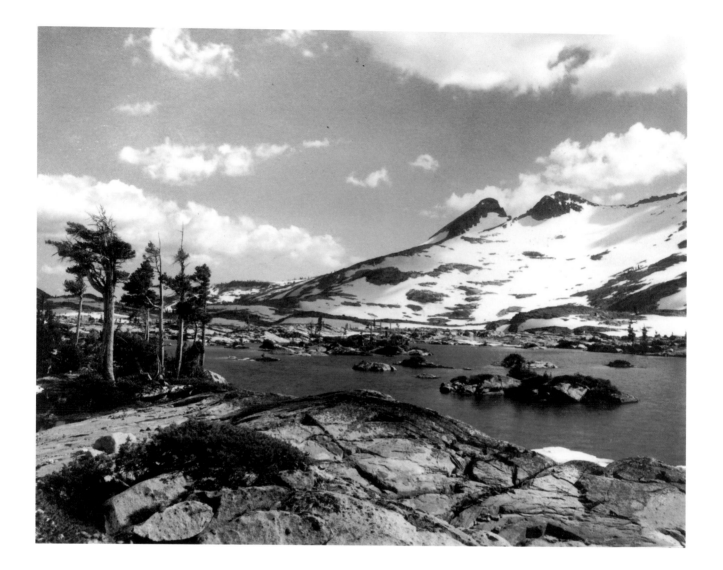

Lake Aloha. Even wilderness areas show evidence of human intervention. The first dam at what is now Lake Aloha was built in 1875. When it was raised in 1917, it transformed the small series of Medley Lakes into the larger Aloha. Located in Desolation Valley within the Desolation Wilderness, it is operated by Pacific Gas and Electric Company, as a storage reservoir to provide hydroelectric power for Sacramento, California. When Desolation Wilderness Area was created in 1969, the power company secured a nonwilderness right-of-way for its dam. The shallow lake is generally empty by mid-September each year, as the water is transferred to reservoirs closer to Sacramento. This view is one-half mile below Lake La Conte.

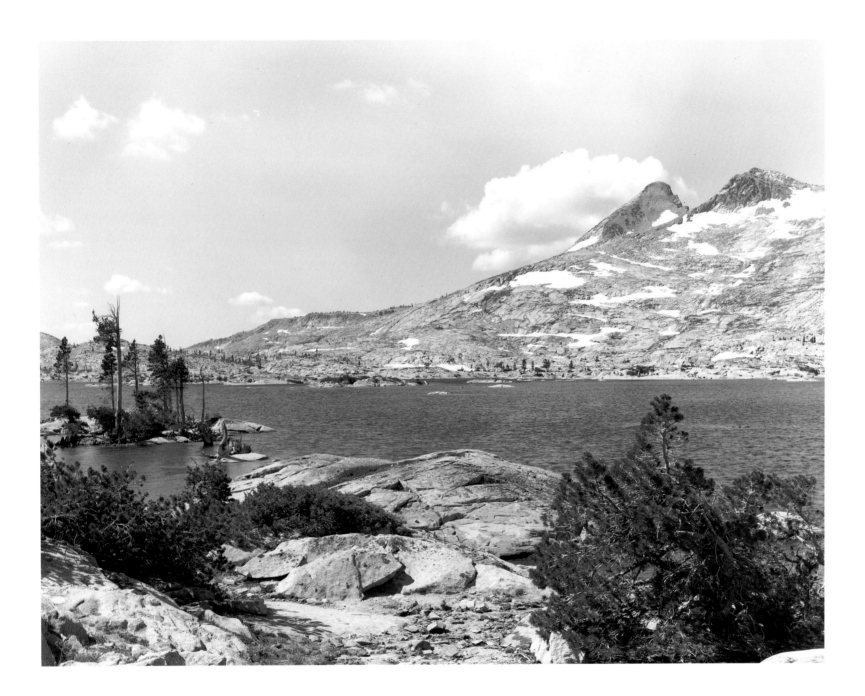

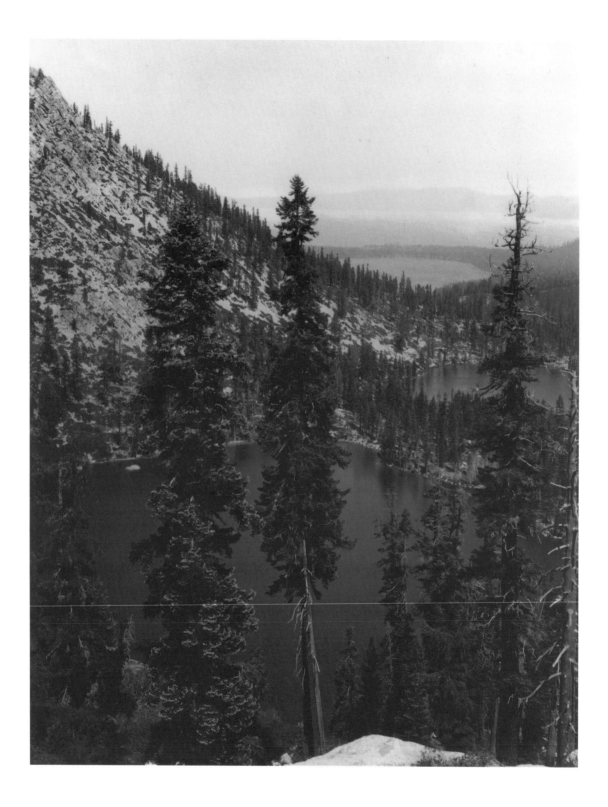

The historical view above shows four lakes—upper Angora, Lower Angora, Fallen Leaf Lake, and Lake Tahoe—in the summer of 1912.

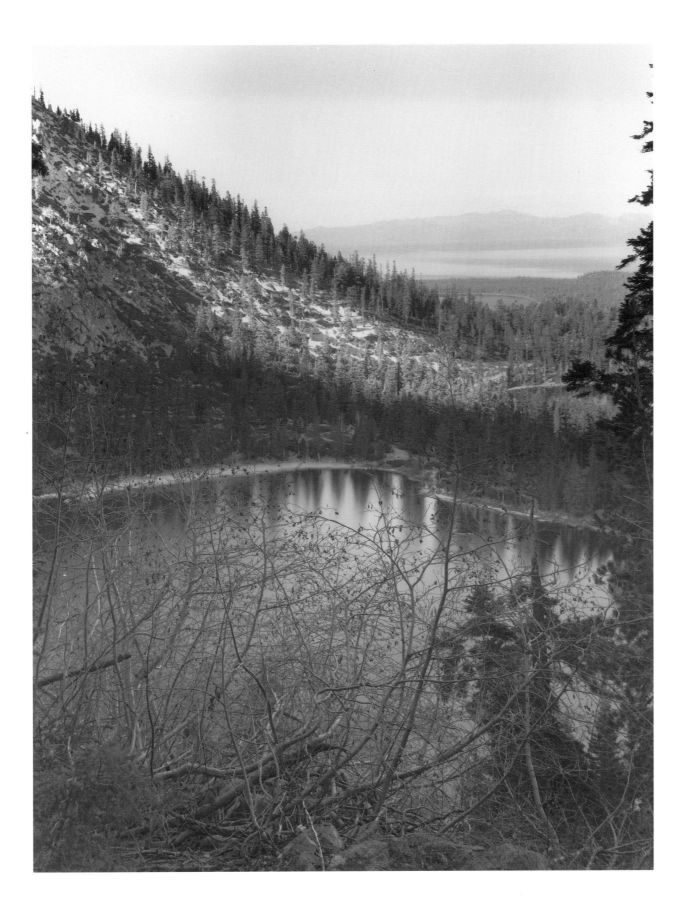

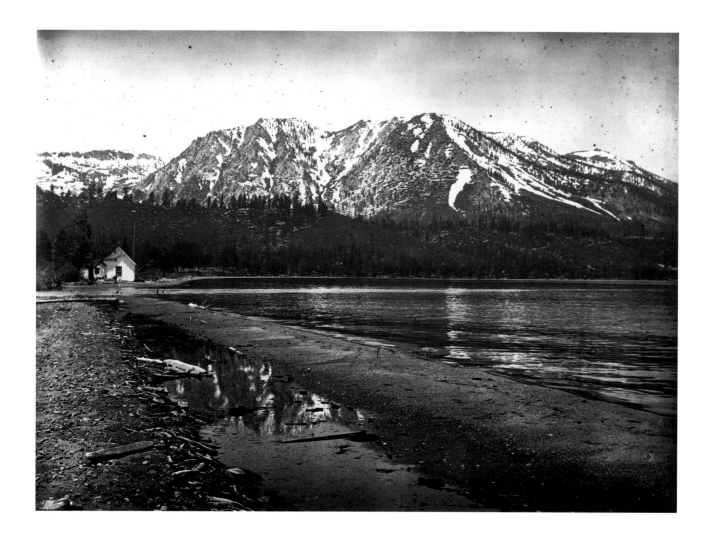

Baldwin Beach. This view of Baldwin Beach/Tallac Beach is at the southern shore of Lake Tahoe, near the site of Lucky Baldwin's luxurious Tallac resort. Beaches like this one were cleared in order to promote recreational use. Baldwin Beach was developed in 1955 and opened to the public in 1956. The U.S. Forest Service manages this area and has encouraged its return to a "natural" state.

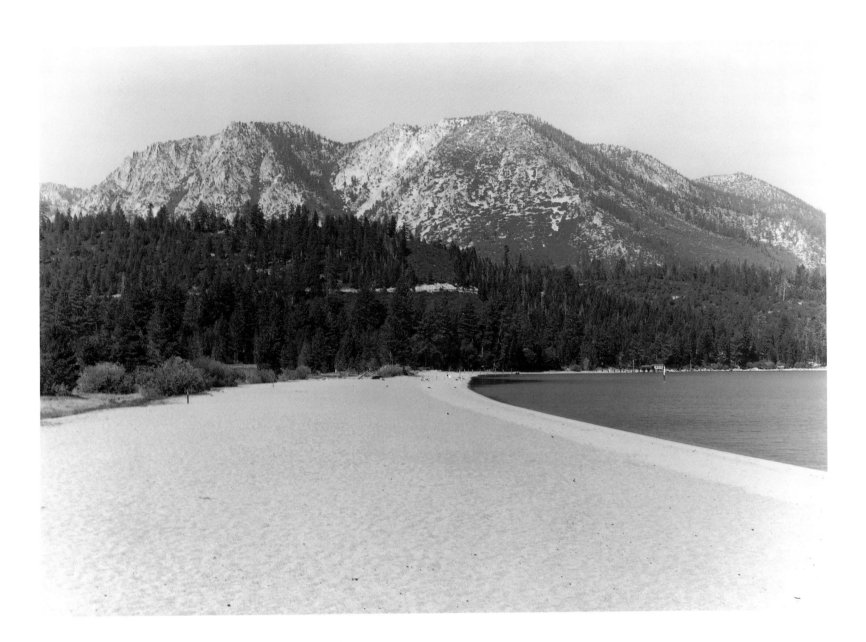

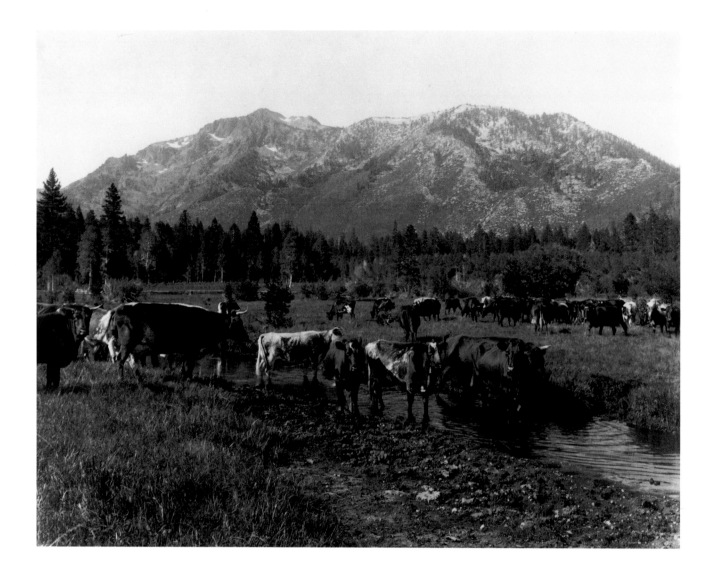

Dairy Meadow. This view of Mt. Tallac and Dairy Meadow suggests the agricultural potential of the Tahoe basin. In the nineteenth century, especially, ranchers took advantage of the rich natural grasses in the mountain meadows throughout the area to feed dairy cattle. When demand dwindled at the turn of the century after the logging camps closed down, beef cattle were substituted. Grazing is no longer permitted in this area managed by the U.S. Forest Service. The stream in the foreground of the historical view (above) is probably Taylor Creek, which has meandered throughout this low-lying marshy area.

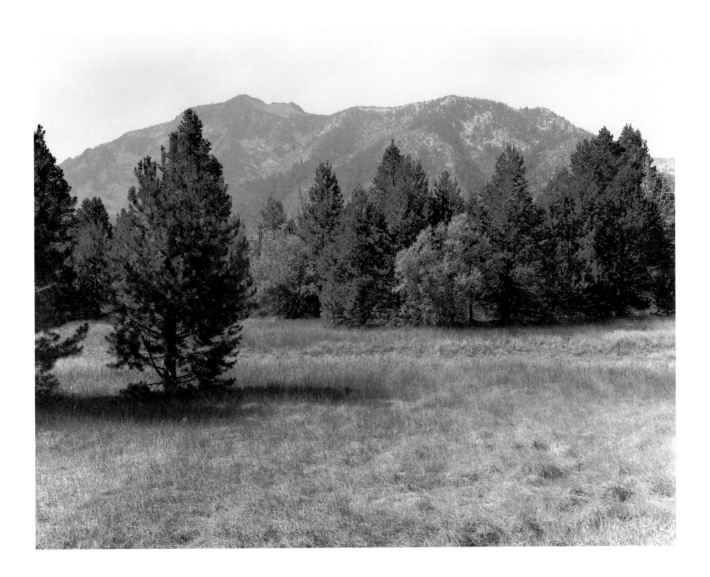

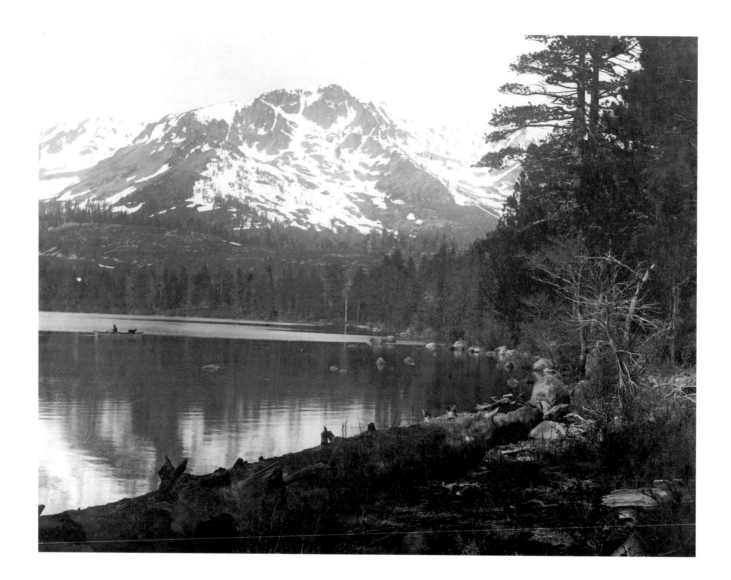

View of Mt. Tallac from Fallen Leaf Lake. Like Cave Rock, Tallac was a noted Tahoe landmark, included on the list of sites that every conscientious tourist should see. The cross of snow, clearly visible in the modern photograph at right, usually remained distinct all summer, and made the slope easy to identify. Photographs of it, some of them hand tinted, were popular souvenirs. The view from the summit of Tallac was magnificent. Yet the ascent also had its more mundane side. In 1877, Nevada journalist Henry Mighels composed a poem while camping on its slopes: "Oh merciless Tallac,/ After many a thump and whack./ I'm astride your rugged back,/ And I am blue and black,/ And limp as any sack./ And yet I'm in the track/Of a most infernal pack,/ Of mosquitoes who attack/My neck about the back. . . ." The modern photograph reflects changes in the lake level and shoreline over time.

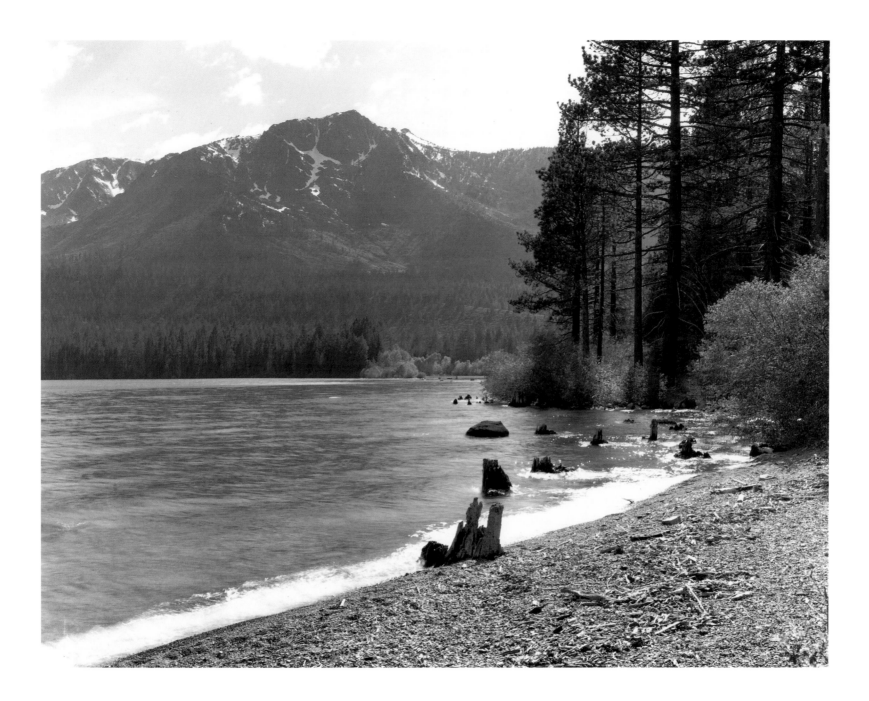

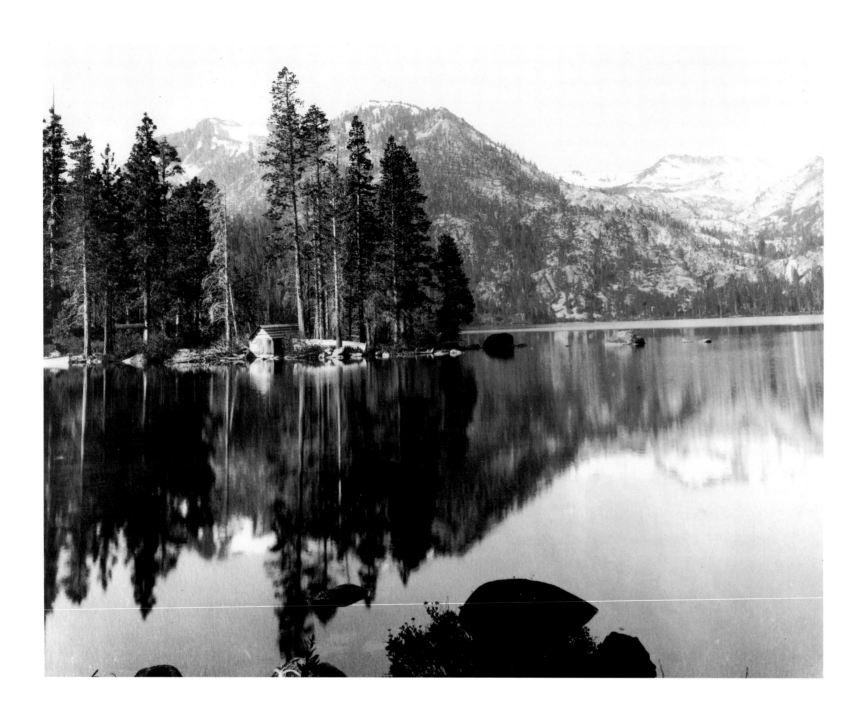

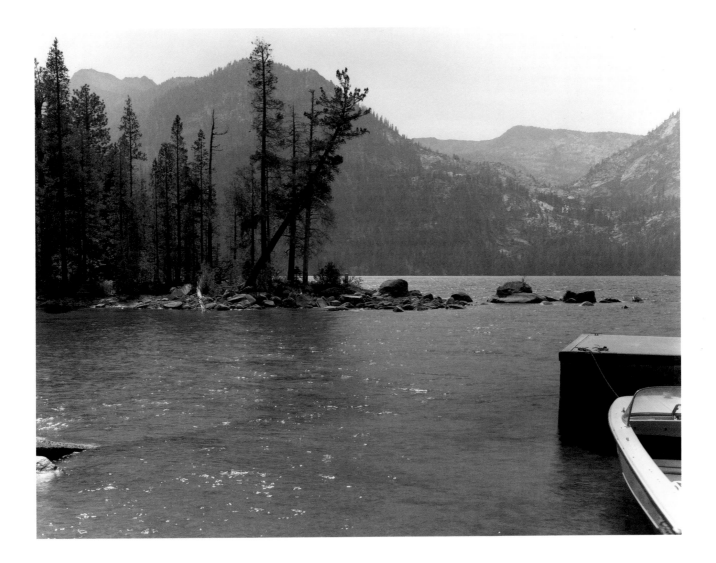

Cascade Lake. All the property around Cascade Lake, near Emerald Bay, is privately leased from the federal government, and public access to the lake is denied. The water in the lake, however, is publicly owned. The historical view (left) shows a boathouse belonging to Dr. Charles Brigham, c. 1886, and suggests the early recreational use of the Tahoe basin, even at the time when it was being logged.

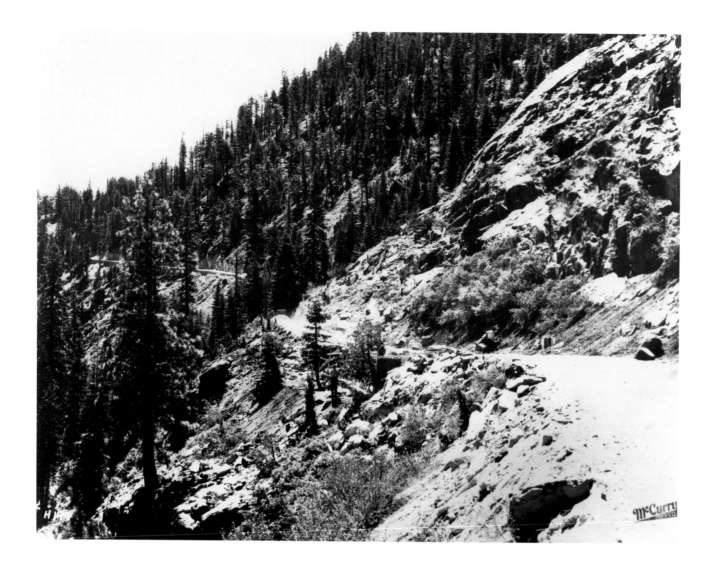

State Route 89 leading to Emerald Bay. Renowned as one of the most beautiful places at Lake Tahoe, Emerald Bay was not on the regular route of many of the early nineteenth-century boats, so it remained somewhat mysterious. Only trails reached the area until the Rim of the Lake Road was completed in 1913. Even today, State Route 89 remains precarious and is frequently closed by winter snows.

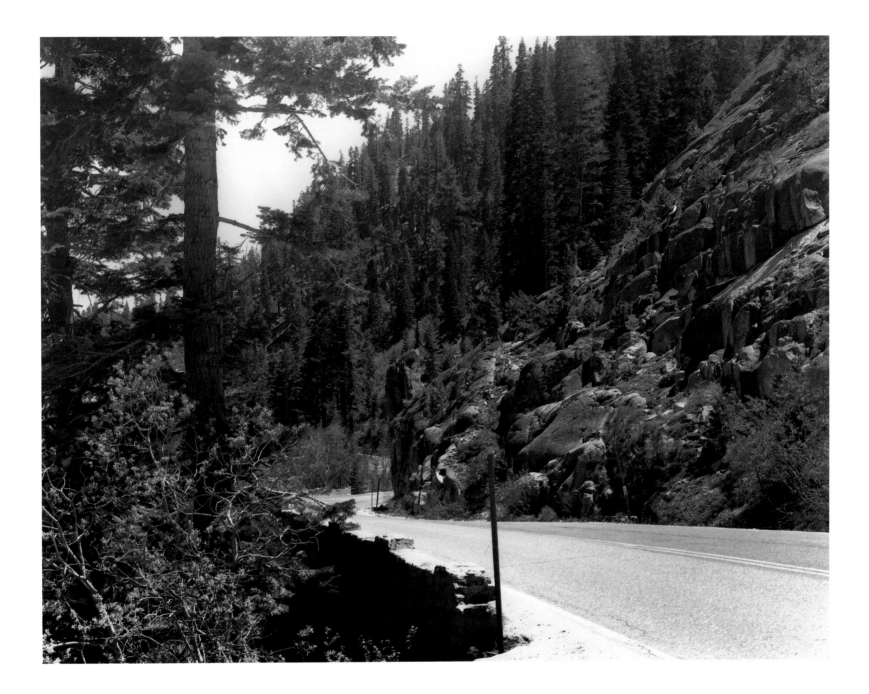

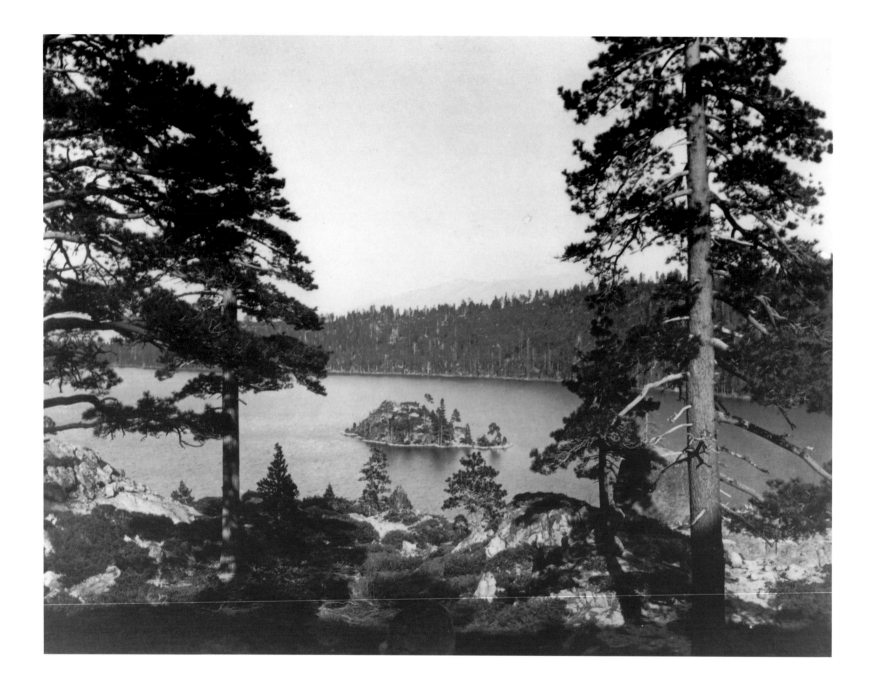

Emerald Bay. This view of Fannette Island in Emerald Bay is across from the entry point to the Desolation Wilderness. The island has a romantic history. In the 1870s an eccentric English sailor named Dick Barter was employed as a caretaker for Ben Holladay, who owned a summer house at Emerald Bay. Barter built a tomb in the rock of the island and announced his intention to be buried in it when he died. Unfortunately, he drowned in the lake in 1873, and his body was never recovered. The tomb remained as a tourist attraction for some years. Later, in 1929, Lora Knight built a

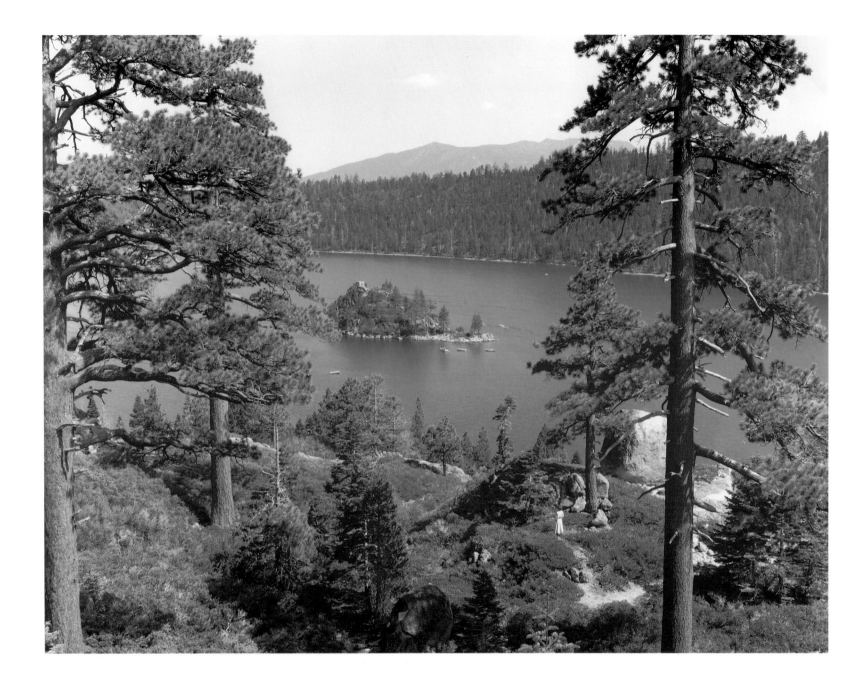

Scandinavian-style home, Vikingsholm, at Emerald Bay. The present stone structure on the island was her tea house. Today the island is a favorite resting spot for recreational boaters at Lake Tahoe.

Because the scale of this photograph is deceptive, the original photographer placed a woman in the foreground facing the lake (left). The modern photograph duplicates this effort in order to point out the location of the woman. Without her figure to provide scale, the rocks and trees appear to be smaller than they actually are.

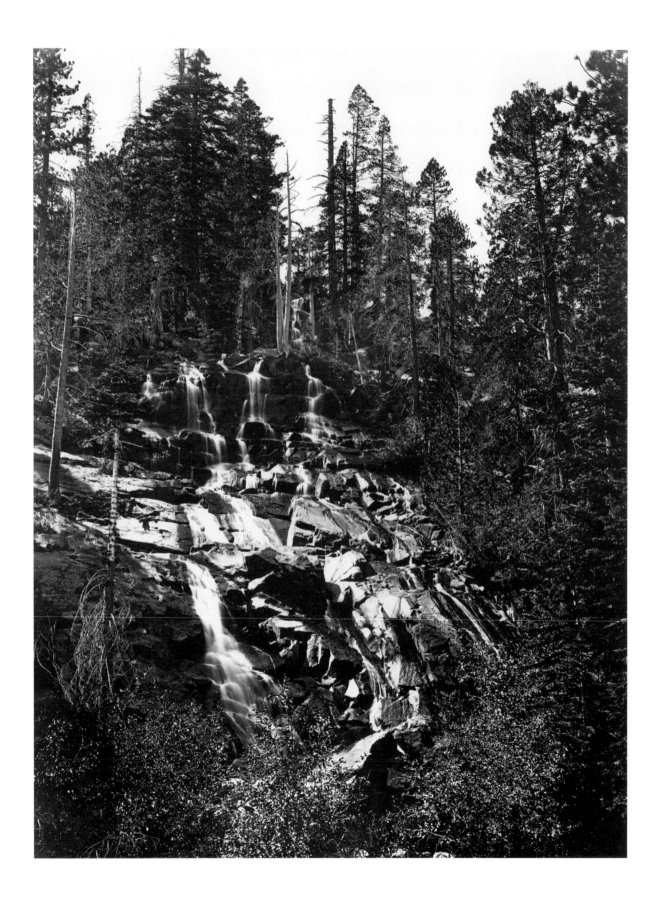

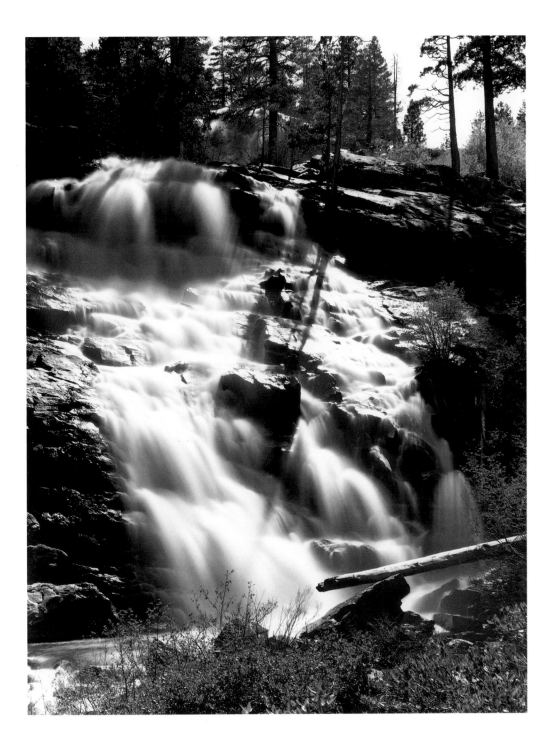

Eagle Falls at Emerald Bay. Occasionally a rephotograph can be misleading. Juxtaposition of this pair suggests that there is more water now in Eagle Falls than there was when the historical image at left was made. Water flow at Tahoe varies with the season, however, and is heavier in the spring than in the fall and winter. Annual precipitation also varies over time, so that periods of heavy snow may be followed by several years of drought. Photographs stop time and capture the look of a landscape at a specific point, but they fail to depict the natural cycles of change that are ongoing over seasons and years.

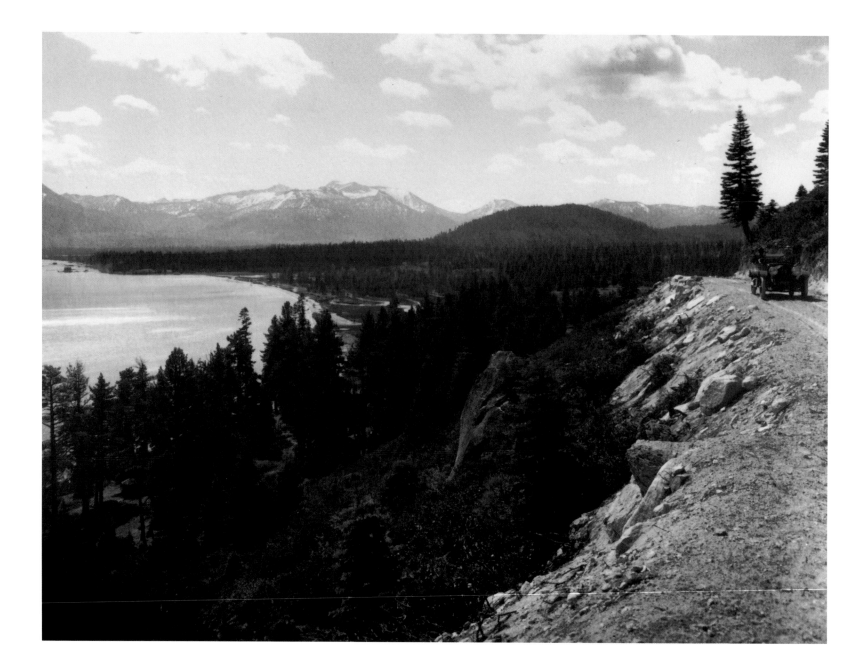

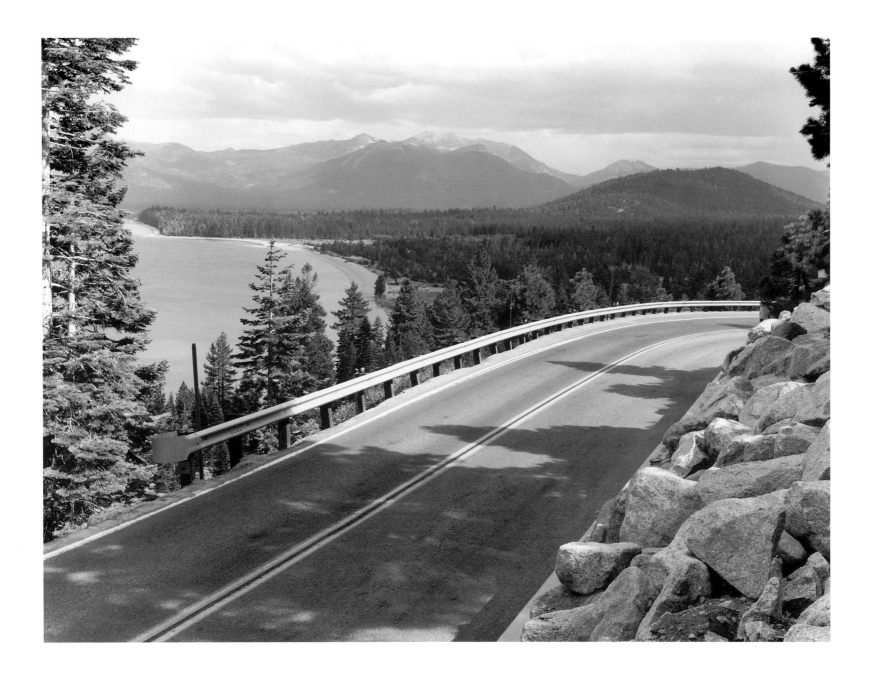

State Route 89 near Emerald Bay. This road leads to the beaches and resort areas at the south end of Lake Tahoe. The entrance to Emerald Bay is hidden between the shoreline and the roadway in the photograph above. The demand for automobile access dictated considerable changes in the landscape. The face of this hillside was dramatically transformed and considerable rock-fill was added to protect the roadway from erosion and avalanches.

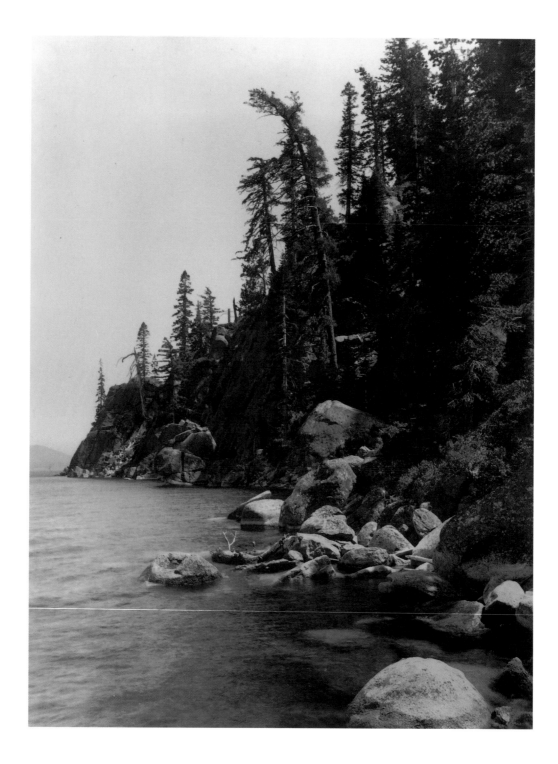

Rubicon Point. Tahoe was most commonly seen from the water during the nineteenth and early twentieth centuries. The limited road system did not provide sufficient opportunity for visitors to see the "best general views" of the area, and most of the earliest accounts of the lake's scenic character were made from boats. These views of Rubicon Point, also made from boats, show how a rock slide has altered the foreground.

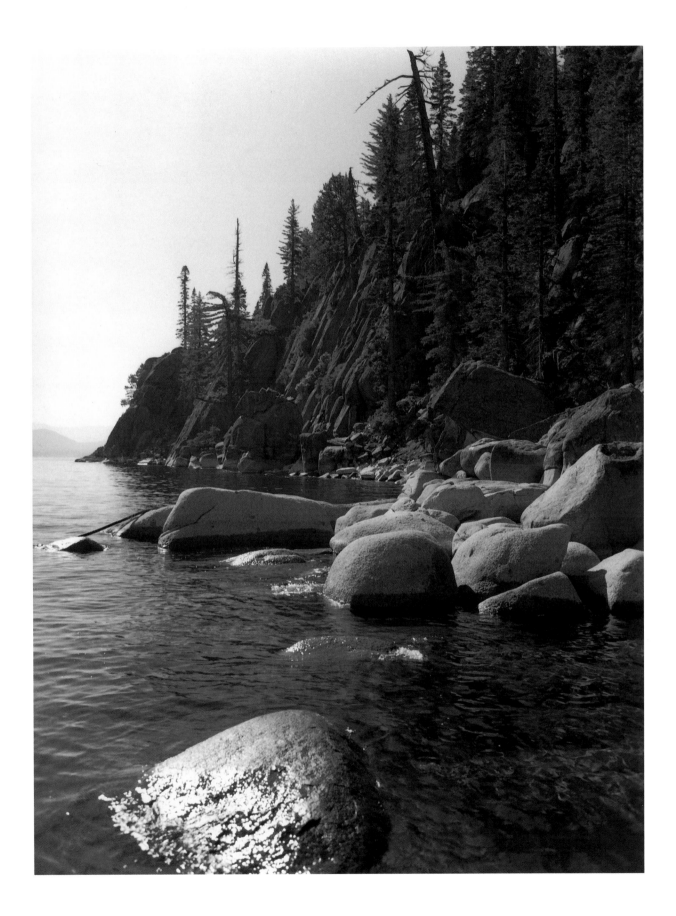

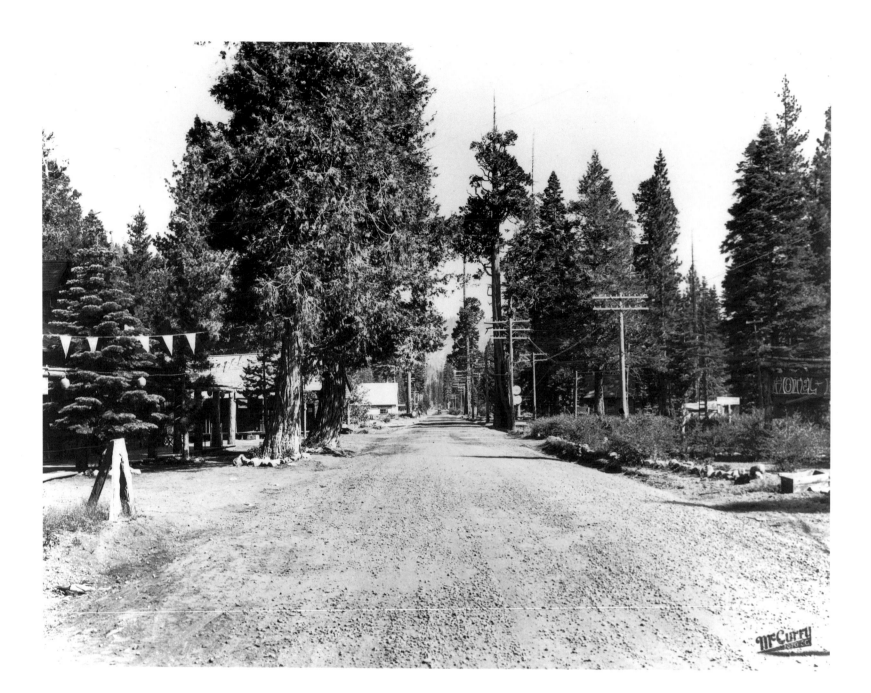

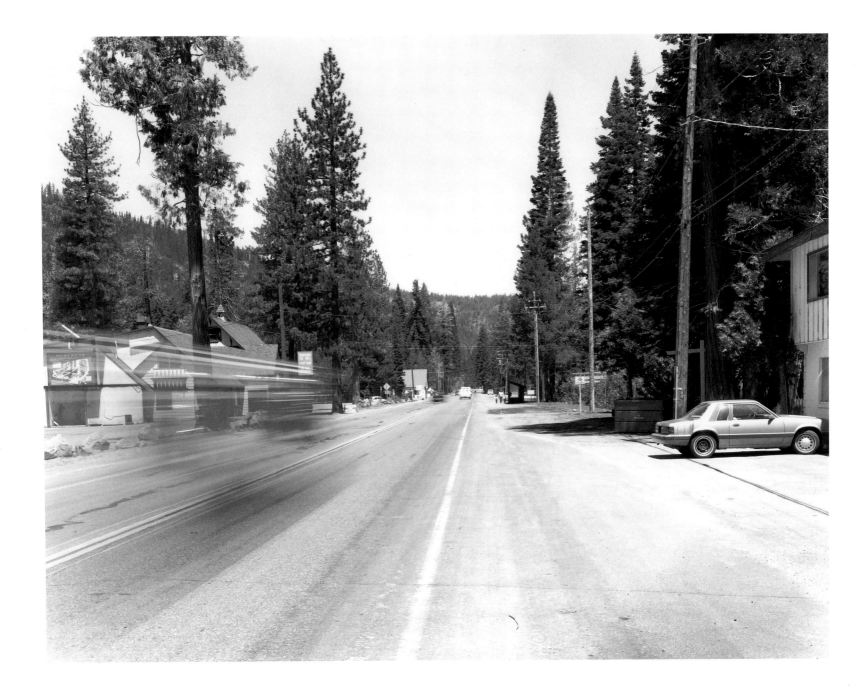

Homewood, California. This view shows State Highway 38 through Homewood in Placer County, California. A small settlement in the early twentieth century, Homewood developed into a family resort by the 1940s. The hotel on the right side of the photograph is present in both views, although more development is evident in the modern view. The Homewood Marina Lodge and the Homewood Ski Area are behind this vantage point.

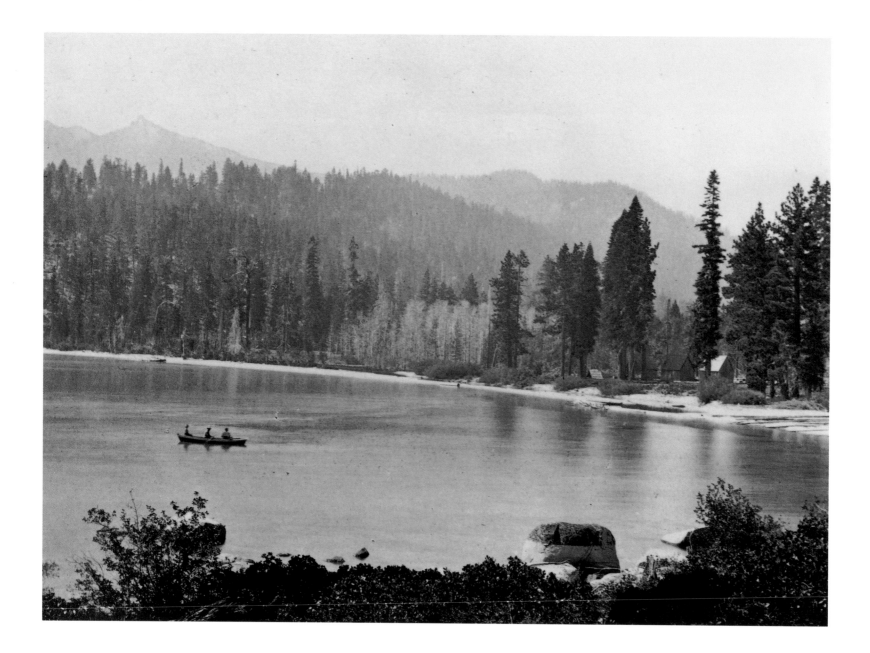

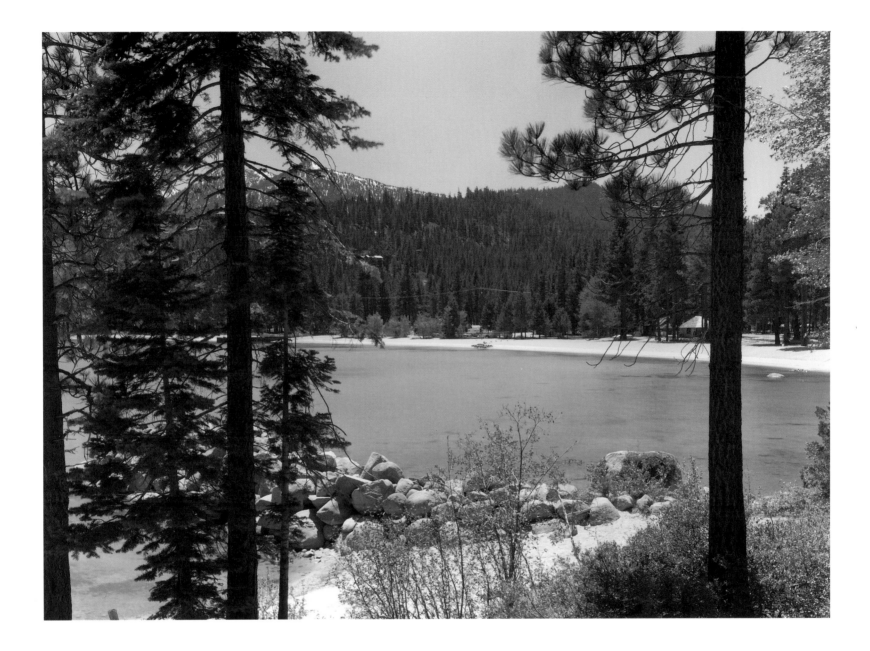

Meeks Bay. This area was a traditional summer campsite for the Washoe, who took advantage of excellent fishing in the bay. It took its name from a haying operation, Meeks & Co., which cut wild hay from the meadows in 1862. Subsequent corruptions of the spelling included Meigs and Meegs. Meeks Bay was the center of western shore lumbering activities of the Carson and Tahoe Lumber and Fluming Company, and the area was logged off by 1884. It became a resort in 1919, featuring a public campground, store, tents, and cabins.

The rock in the foreground is the same in both images, but the new growth of trees behind the vantage point made finding the exact spot for rephotography impossible.

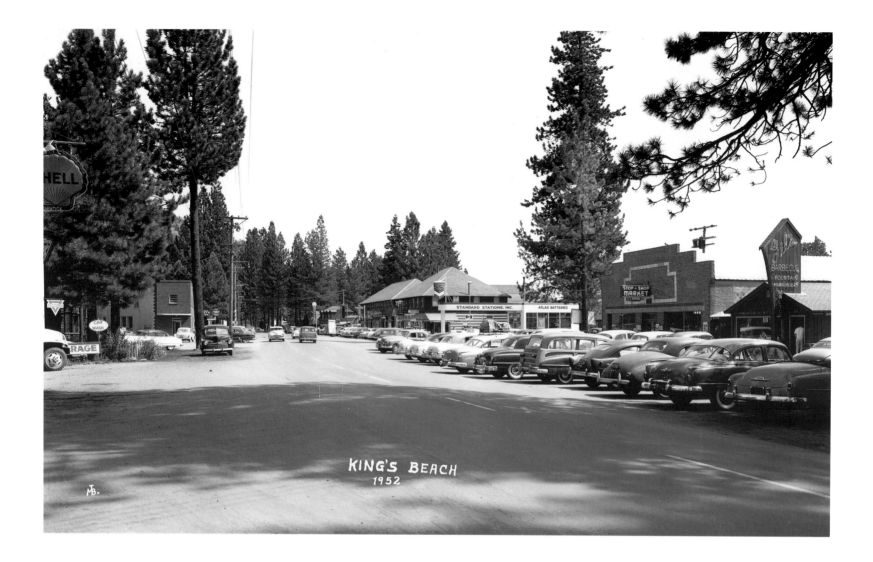

KING'S BEACH
1952

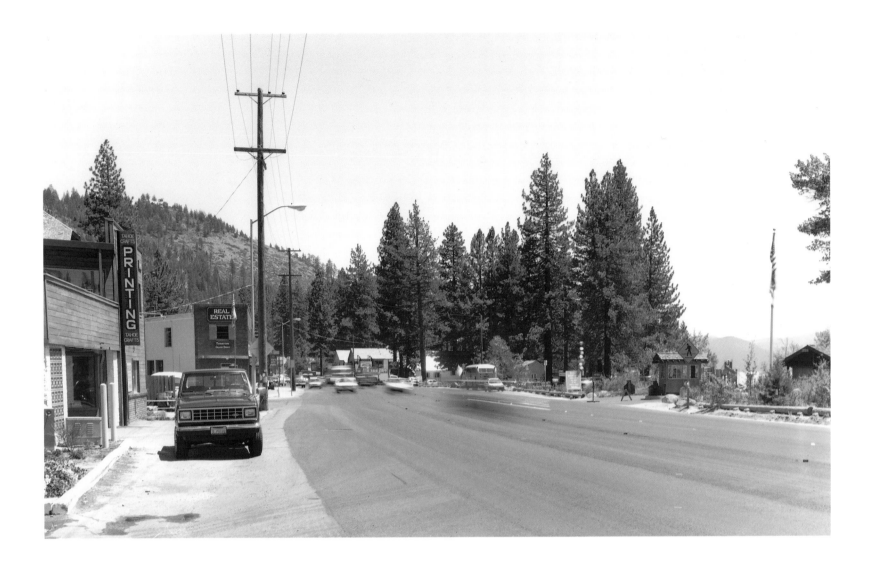

King's Beach. Sometimes the direction of environmental change at Tahoe is surprising. The commercial establishments on the right side of the historical photograph, which once earned the area the reputation of being Lake Tahoe's Coney Island, were replaced by King's Beach State Recreation Area after the site was acquired from the King Estate in 1974. The real estate office is the same building in both photographs, the only absolute clue to the original vantage point. The hillside is hidden behind the trees in the historical view, on the left.

King's Beach. Taken in 1944 by Michael T. Benning, the photographs of King's Beach at right provide comparative evidence of the development of beaches as recreational sites. The view of King's Beach from a boat, above, was made c. 1950. It suggests the popularity of Tahoe as a recreational site.

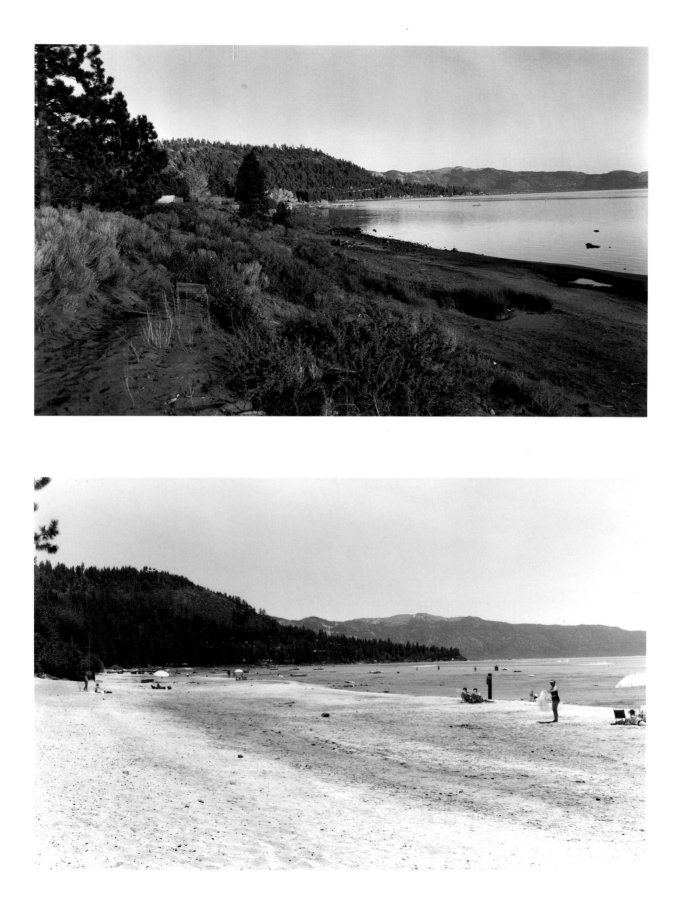

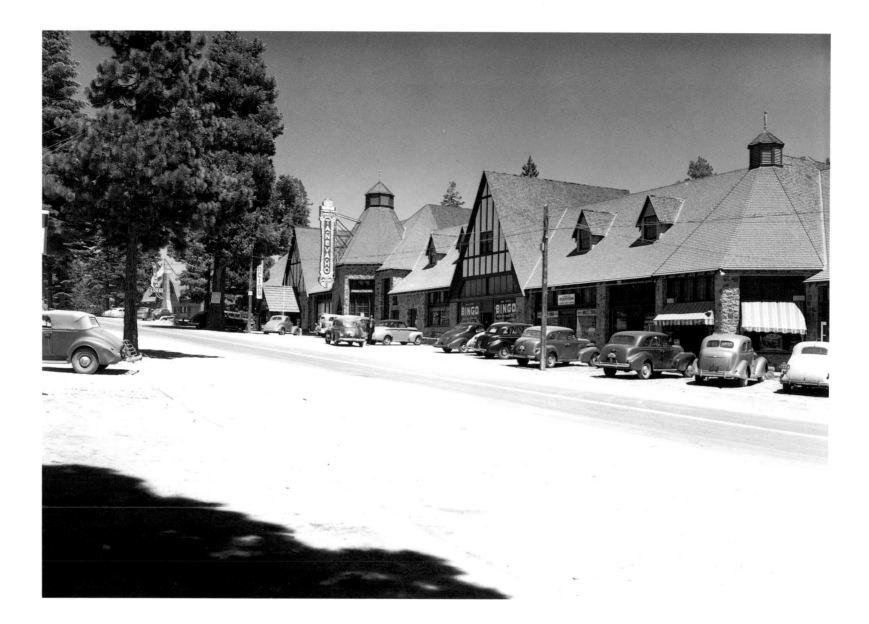

Crystal Bay. The Ta-Ne-Va-Ho, abridged from Tahoe and Nevada, has become the Crystal
Bay Club and Casino. Located at the north boundary between Nevada and California, the
modern casino reflects its architectural heritage. The old roofline and cupola have been
incorporated into the expanded modern structure.

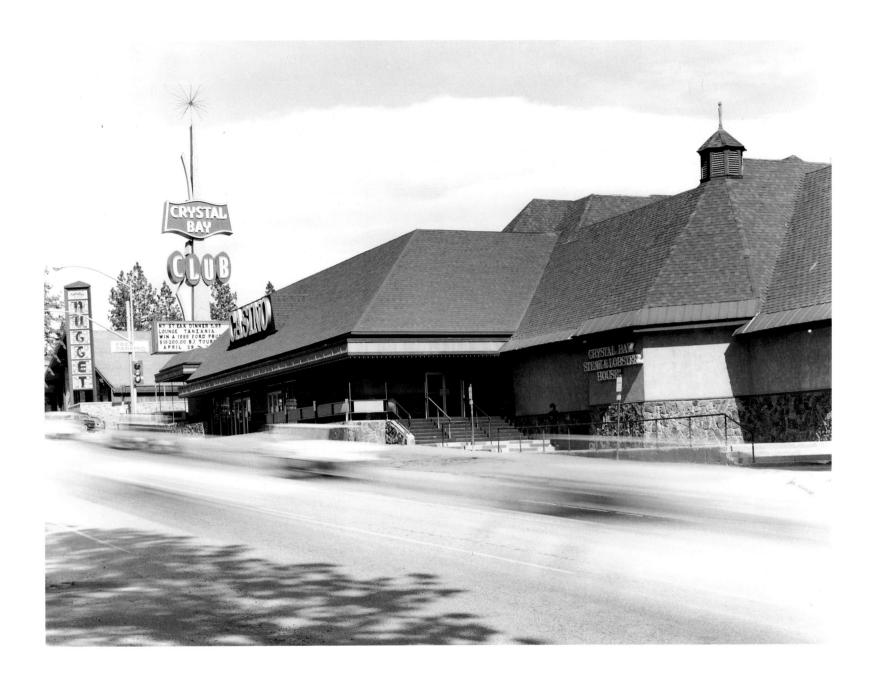

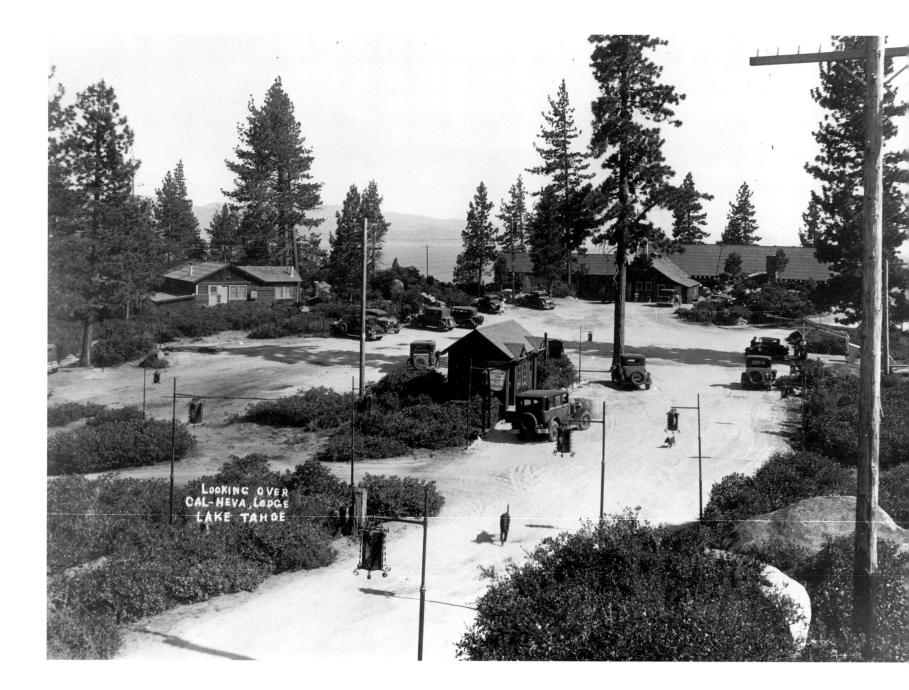

Looking Over
Cal-Neva, Lodge
Lake Tahoe

Crystal Bay. The evolution of the parking lot at the Cal-Neva Lodge reflects an increasing concern for the utilization of space and accommodation of automobiles over the preservation of a natural environment. The state boundary runs through the middle of the Cal-Neva Lodge, which was originally built in the 1920s by Robert Sherman of San Francisco. In 1930, after its sale to notorious Reno underworld figures James McKay and William Graham, it was operated as a night club and casino. The original lodge burned and was rebuilt in 1937. In the early 1960s it was owned by Frank Sinatra. The contemporary view (bottom right) was taken from a raised area next to the road, site of the Tahoe Tour and Travel Bureau.

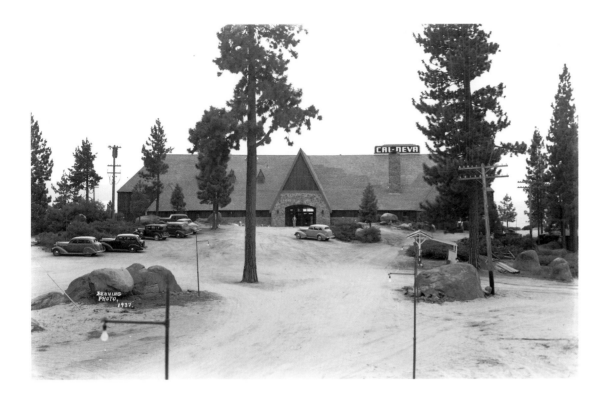

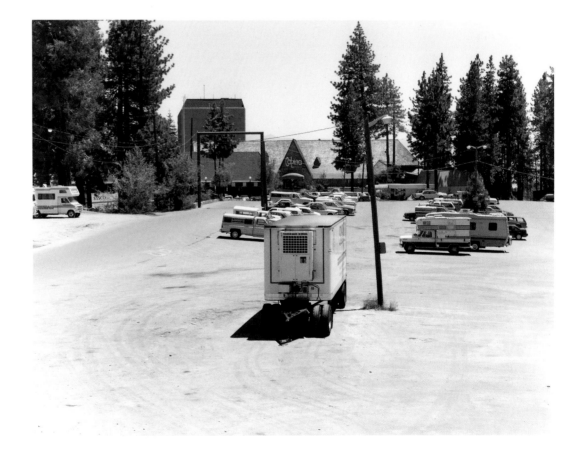

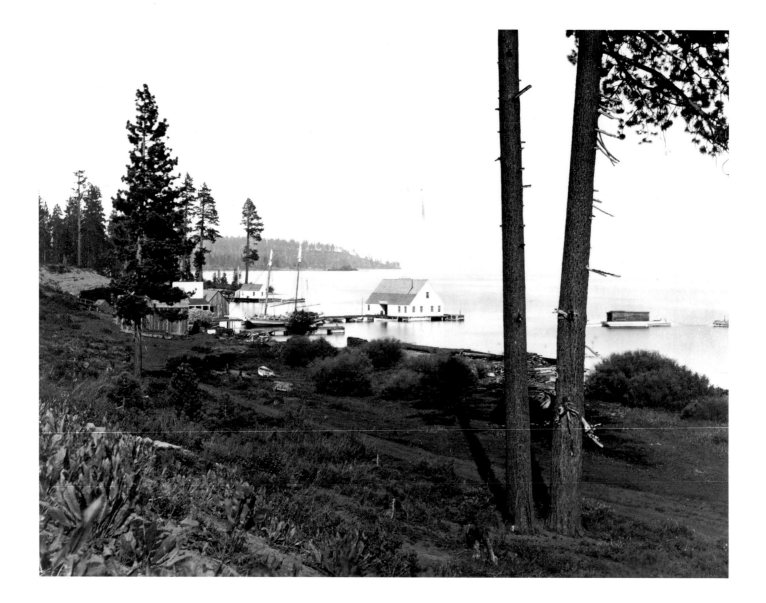

Tahoe City, California. The Custom House Wharf is partially obscured in the contemporary rephotograph (right) of the original 1872 view. The original photograph, above, reflects an era when steamers were the primary means of transportation at Lake Tahoe, and wharves were the point of embarkation. The modern park, named the "Commons Beach," was established along a strip of shoreline that was confirmed by Congress in 1868 as part of Tahoe City.

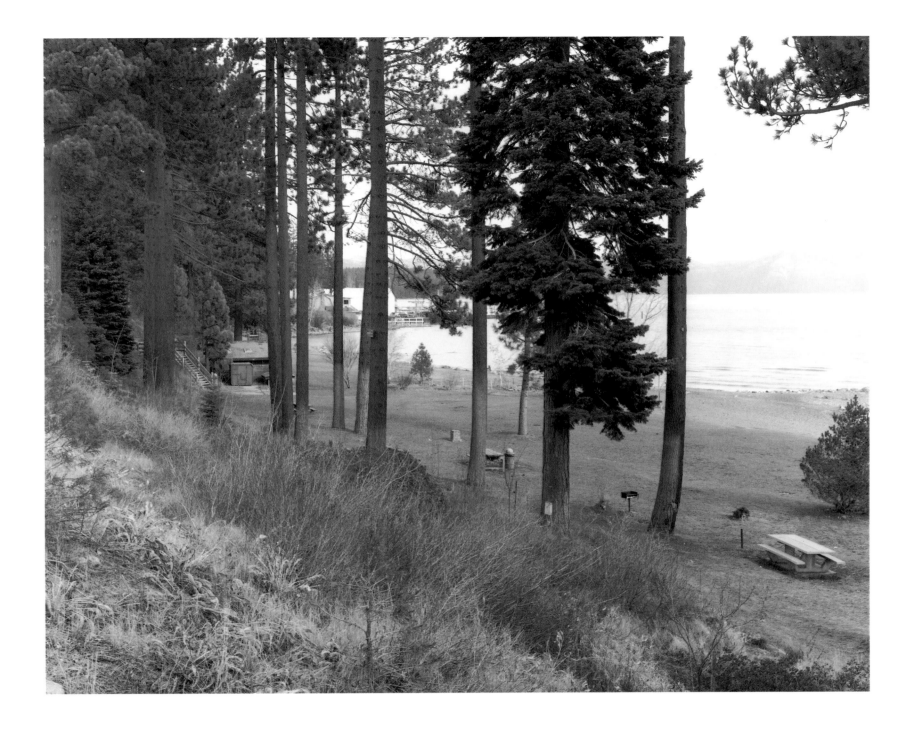

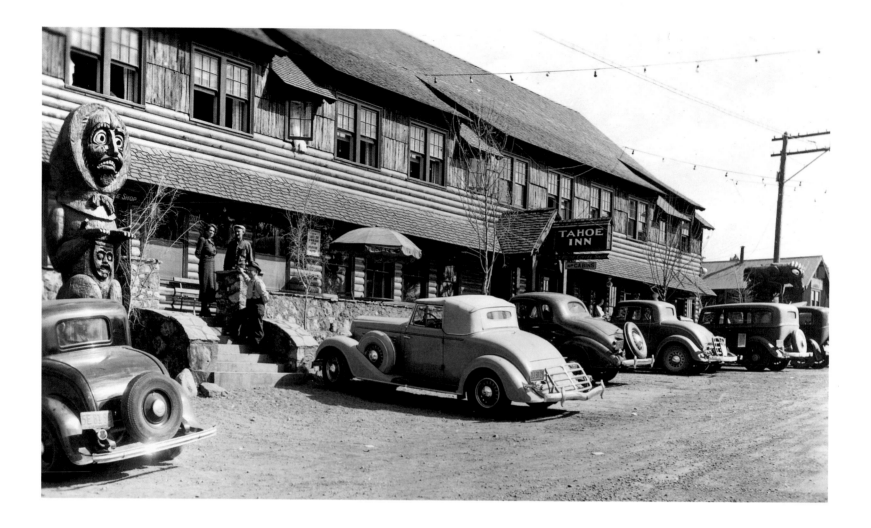

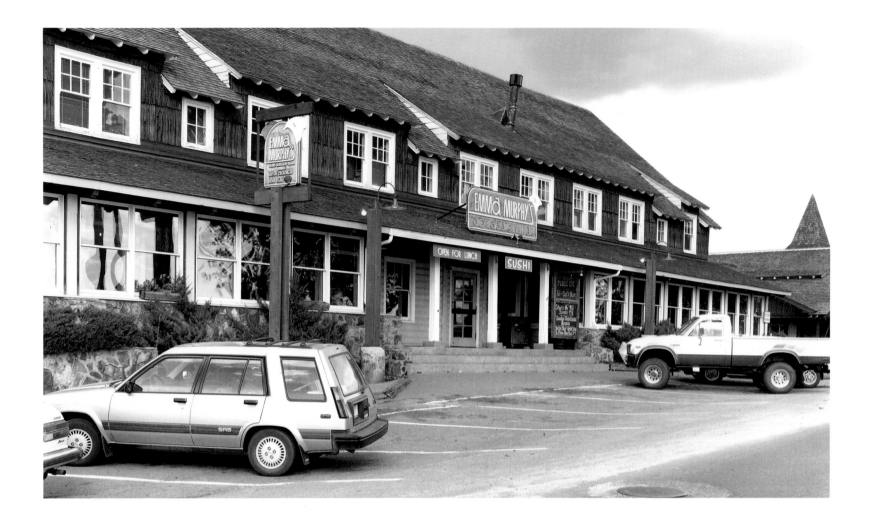

Tahoe City. Commercial establishments in the Tahoe basin have traditionally adopted a rustic, wood-shingled style that is reflective of their natural setting. Although the Tahoe Inn has undergone a metamorphosis to "Emma Murphy's and the Avalanche Sushi Bar," the building is clearly the same.

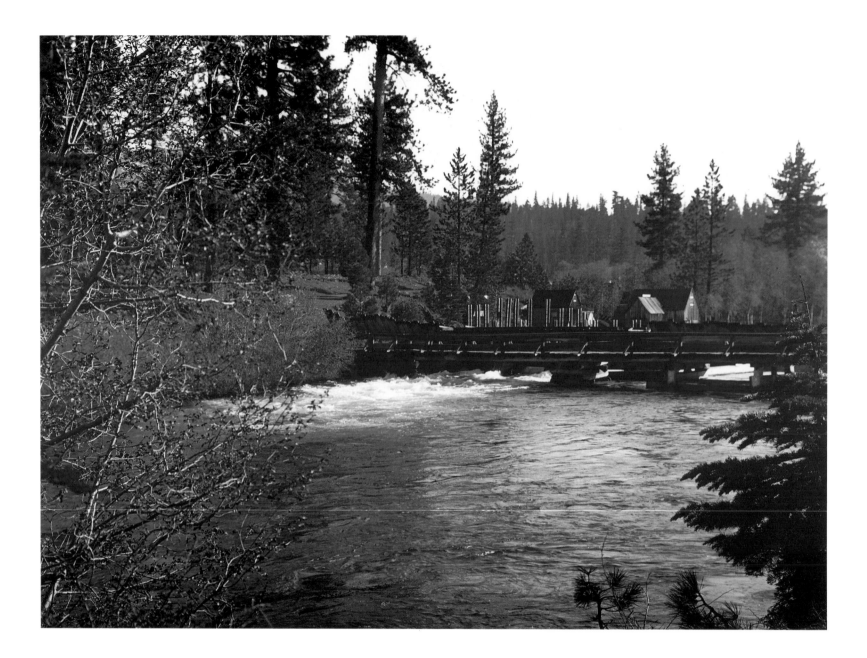

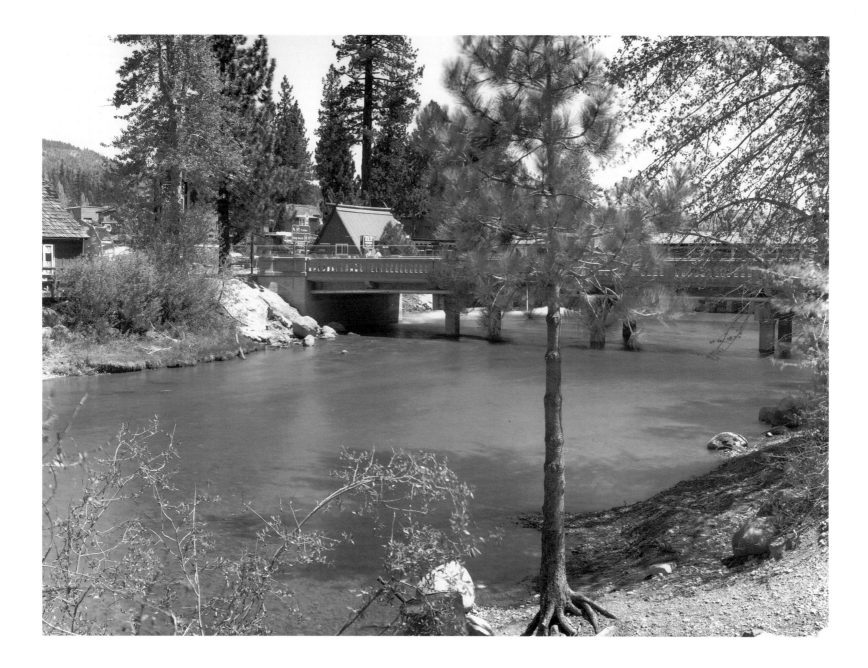

Tahoe City. The historical view at left, taken in 1906, shows the wooden outlet dam that was originally proposed by von Schmidt as part of his ambitious plan to provide water for San Francisco. The modern bridge, completed in 1913, spans the Truckee River just down-stream. It is familiarly known as the "Fanny Bridge" because the posteriors of pedestrians are frequently displayed as they lean over to view the lake's modern outlet dam.

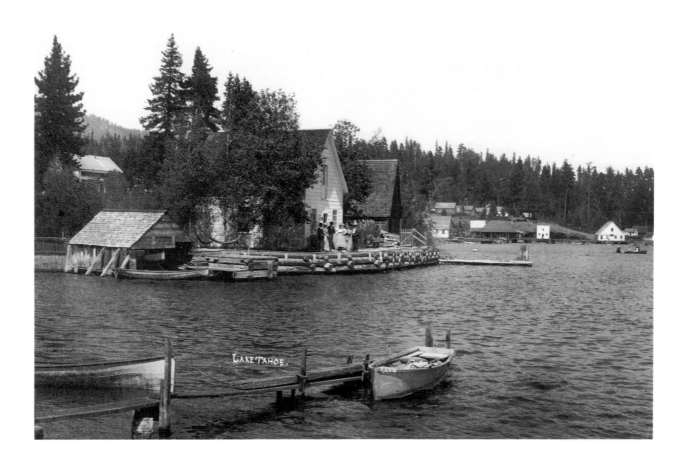

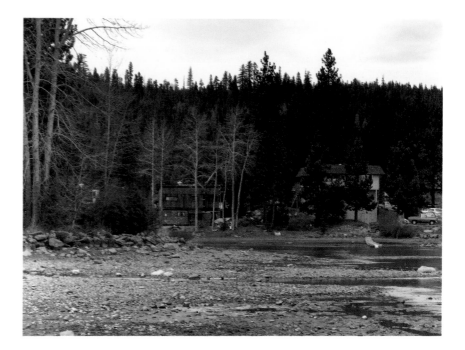

Tahoe City. Originally photographed by Reno photographer William Cann in 1901, these views of the Truckee River outlet from Lake Tahoe provide an excellent example of the dramatic landscape changes typical of the Tahoe basin. The modern triptych encompasses an area greater than the original view, but it demonstrates the low water level and landfill condominiums that now define the same space. In drought years, when the full amount of water stored in Lake Tahoe has been drained for downstream use, the Truckee River ceases to flow altogether. By federal mandate, intended in part to protect property owners at Tahoe, the lake level is maintained at its natural rim, 6,223 feet above sea level.

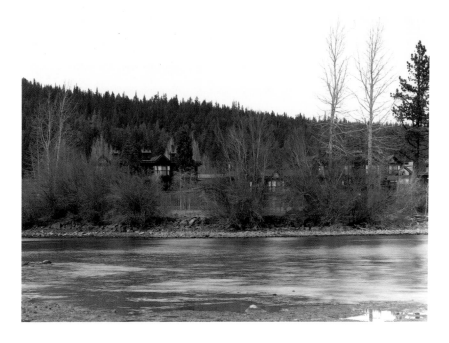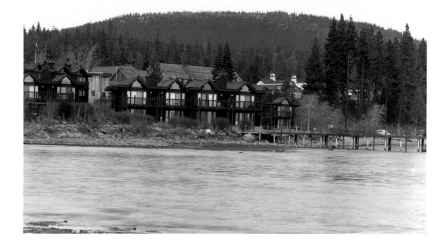

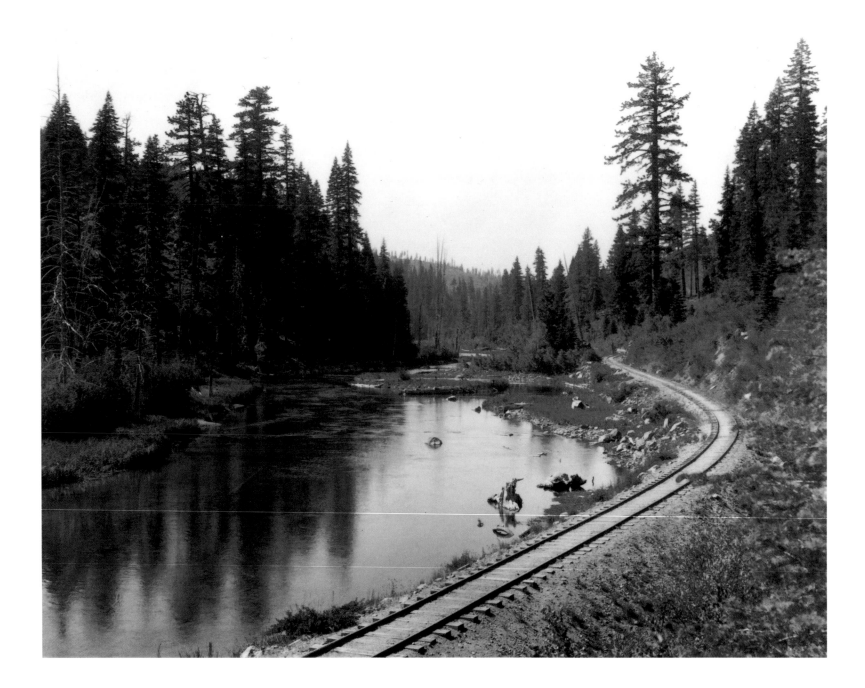

Truckee River Canyon. This route—from the railroad at Truckee, California, to the lake at Tahoe City—was the customary approach for tourists before automobiles were common. Early visitors made the trip in wagons or carriages, or on horseback. The railroad in the historical photograph (left) was built by the Bliss family of the Carson and Tahoe Lumber and Fluming Company, to serve their new resort at Tahoe City, the Tahoe Tavern. It began operation in 1900, and was scrapped during World War II. It has been replaced in the modern photograph with a bicycle path.

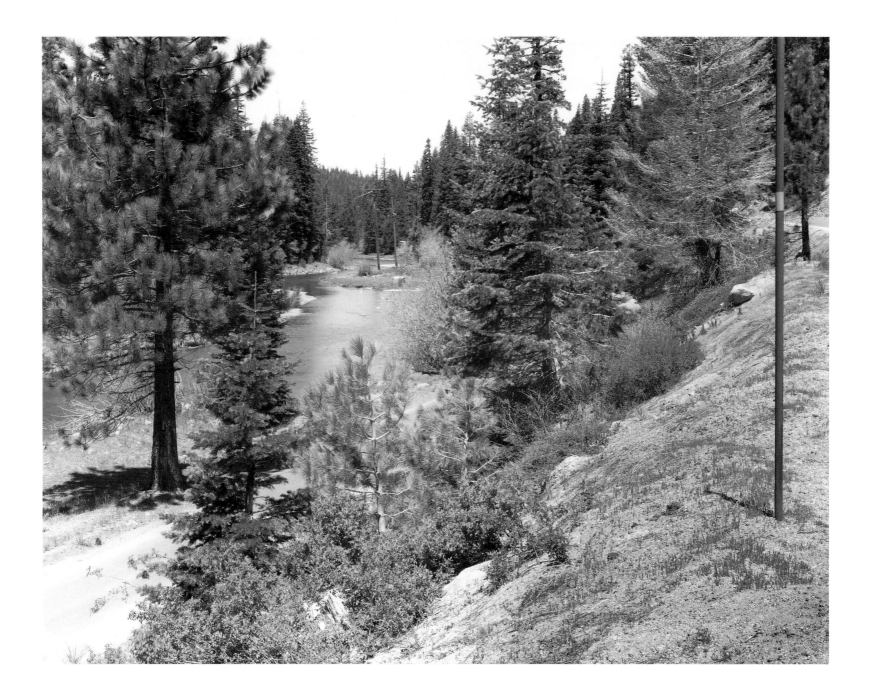

The vegetation nearly obscures the horizon in the modern photograph. This site is located approximately one-fourth mile before the "National Forest Lands, Lake Tahoe Basin" sign on Highway 89, just past the Alpine Meadows Ski Area and the River Ranch Resort. The overgrowth, lack of landmarks, and minimal horizon made this one of the most difficult sites to find and rephotograph.

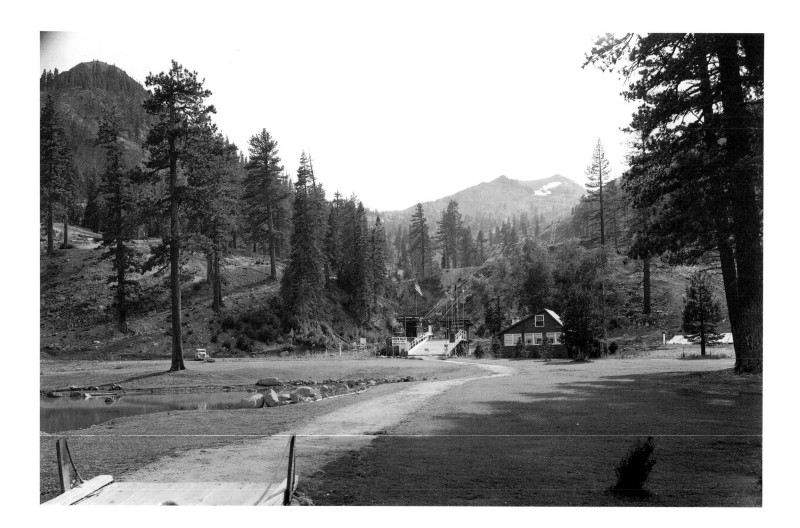

Squaw Valley. Historically an important summer gathering site for the Washoe, Squaw Valley was the site of a brief mining boom in 1863, and then was used for summer range for livestock. In 1949, the Squaw Valley Development Corporation was formed, and a modern ski lodge and runs were constructed. In 1955, Squaw Valley was designated as the site for the 1960 winter Olympics. The attention focused on Lake Tahoe by this event was responsible for the tremendous growth of winter skiing and the expansion of the tourist industry in the Tahoe basin.

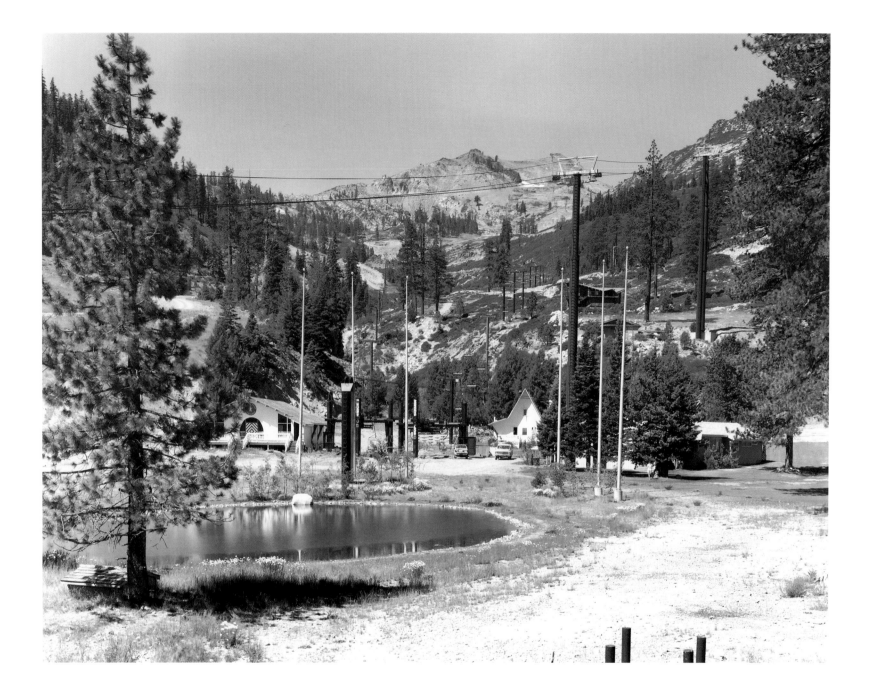

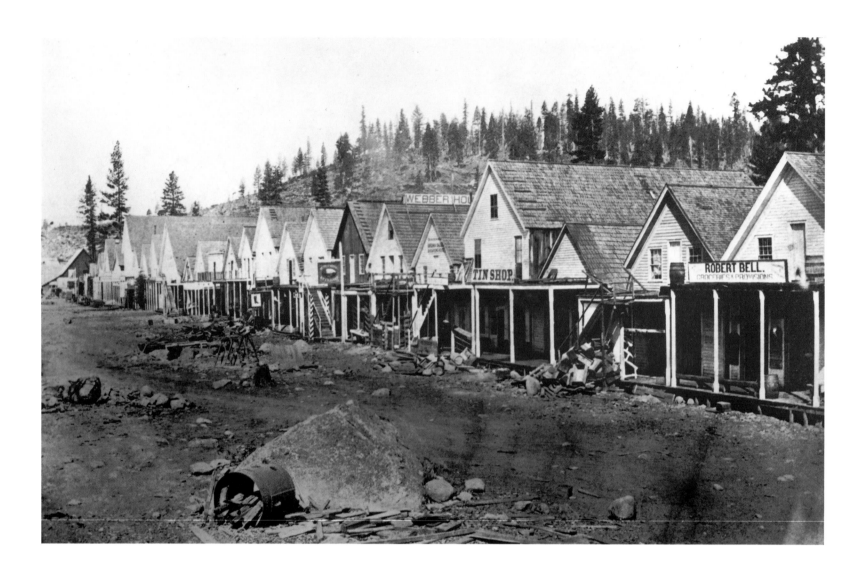

Truckee, California. Although there was a stage stop in this vicinity by 1863, the town of Truckee was established by the Central Pacific Railroad in 1868. By virtue of its location, Truckee became the most common departure point for people making the journey to Lake Tahoe. It was also an important lumber milling town. One journalist who visited it in 1870, about the time of the historical photograph, was not favorably impressed by what he saw. His report to the San Francisco *Alta California* described Truckee as "a straggling town of some 120 inhabitants [that] wears a dilapidated appearance, as if it had outlived its usefulness. Several sawmills are in active operation, giving employment to a portion of the population: the rest stand around and see the others work."

In the nineteenth century, Truckee was a boisterous town of saloons, the place where lumbermen spent their pay and whiled away their leisure hours. The modern community is a resort center, with lodging, restaurants, bars, and boutiques catering to winter skiers and summer tourists.

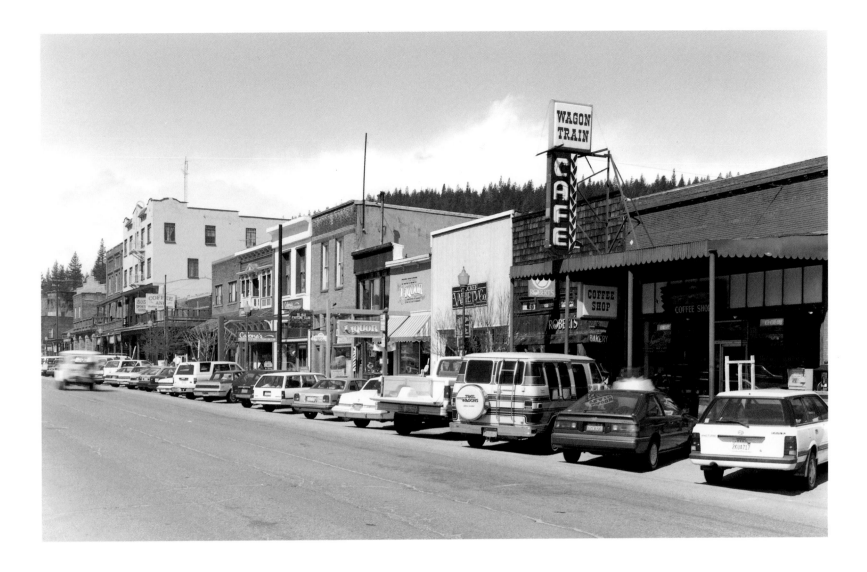

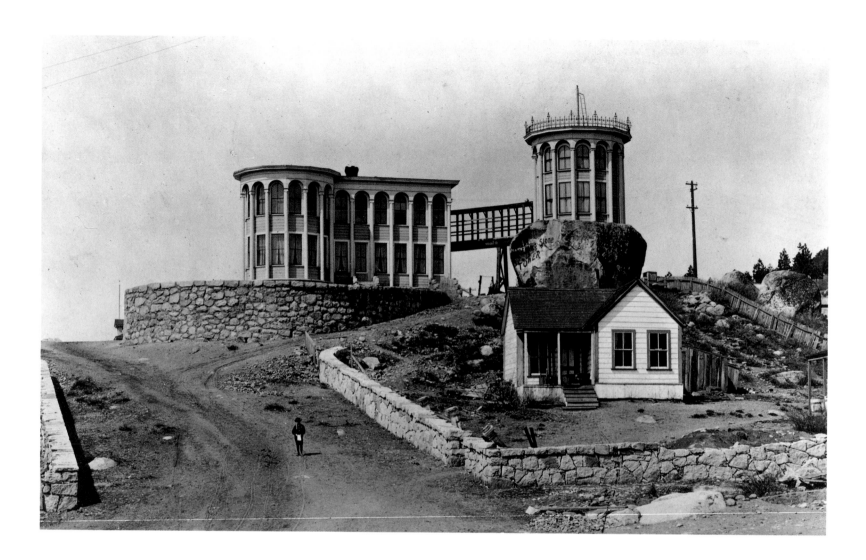

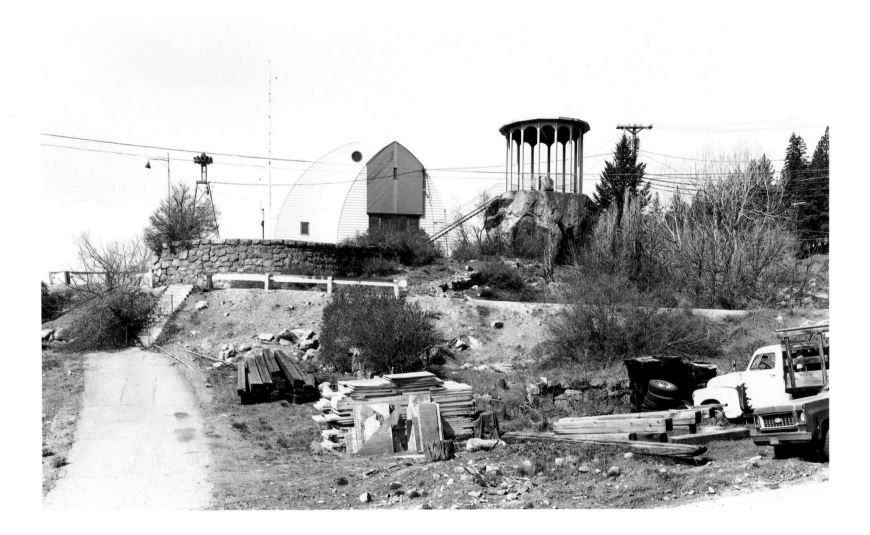

Truckee. This mansion was built in 1903 by Charles F. McGlashan, attorney, editor of the Truckee *Republican*, former California state assemblyman, and advocate of official protection for the site where the Donner Party had wintered in 1846. He built the Rocking Stone Tower, to the right of his home, in 1893, in order to protect that natural phenomenon. The house burned in 1935, and is now the site of the Veterans Memorial Building. The remnants of the Rocking Stone Tower, however, remain a landmark for passing motorists along Interstate Highway 80.

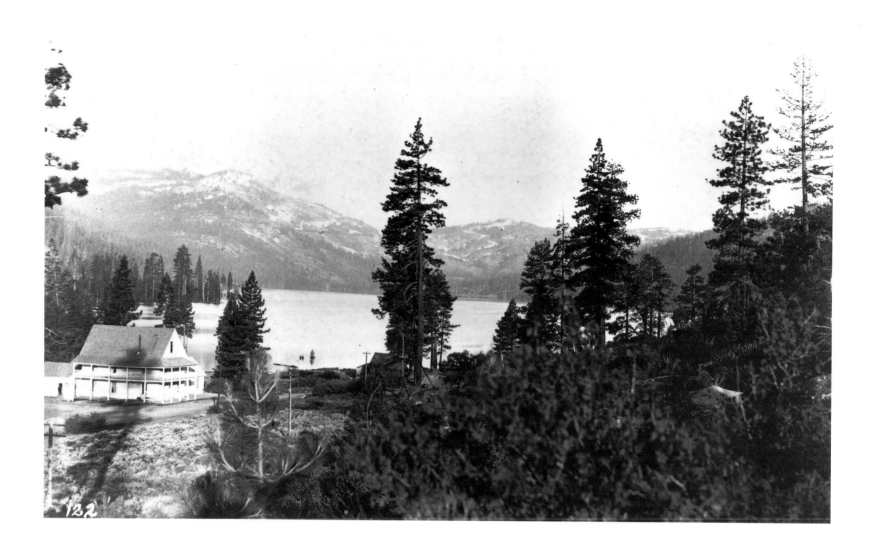

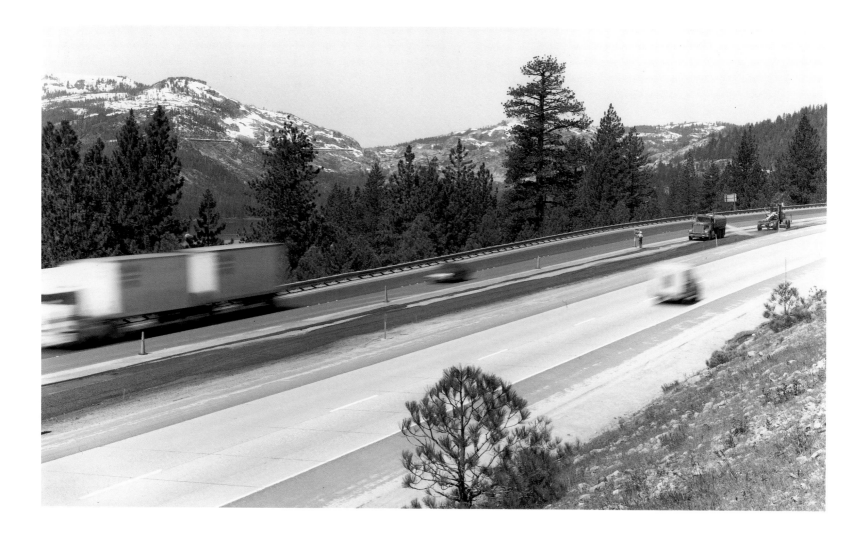

Donner Lake. Known as Truckee Lake in the 1850s and 1860s, this lake was officially called Donner by the 1876 Wheeler Survey. While attempting to reach California, the infamous Donner Party was trapped along its shores by early winter storms in 1846. Many members of the group perished during the ensuing winter, and some were forced to resort to cannibalism before they were rescued in the spring. Their unfortunate circumstances cast a pall over the Truckee River route, and subsequent emigrant parties preferred to cross the formidable Sierra Nevada by other routes. The Emigrant Trail Museum dedicated to their memory is located in California's Donner Memorial State Park at the eastern end of the lake.

The construction of Interstate Highway 80 has completely obscured the historical view of Donner Lake. This was a very difficult view to find due to the foreground changes created by the interstate and the forest growth. The tree in the center of the historical photograph is present, but obscured in the rephotograph. The site of the historical hotel building is now the Tahoe-Donner Marina, reserved for private members.

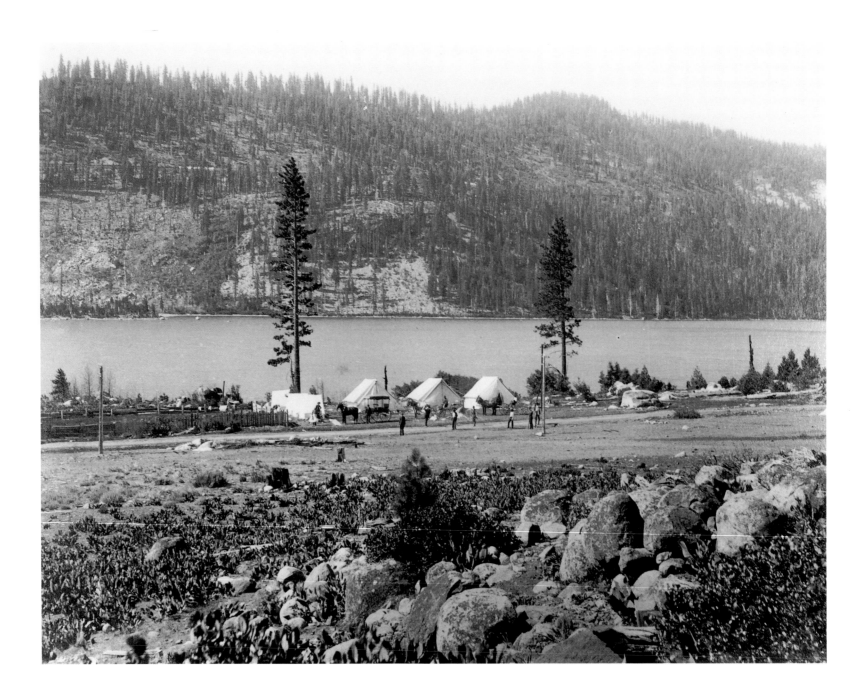

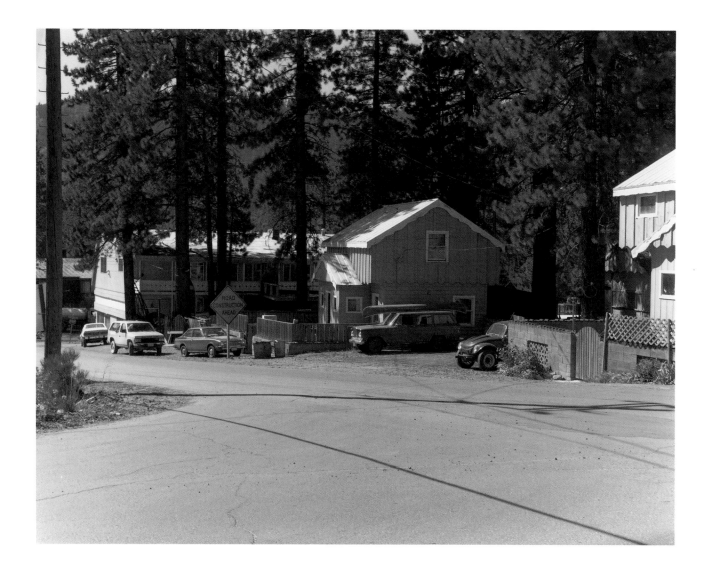

Camp Powell, Donner Lake. Many private homes now occupy the site of the isolated and temporary Camp Powell at Donner Lake. The exact vantage point is nearly impossible to find amidst the closely clustered structures that now surround the lake.

Donner Lake was a popular resort during the nineteenth century, when winter skating and sledding parties were held along its shores. It was the subject of a painting by renowned landscape artist Thomas Moran, and was preferred over Lake Tahoe by several nineteenth-century guidebooks. Its visibility from the route of the Central Pacific Railroad meant that many travelers who did not detour to see Lake Tahoe had glimpsed Donner Lake from the windows of their railroad cars.

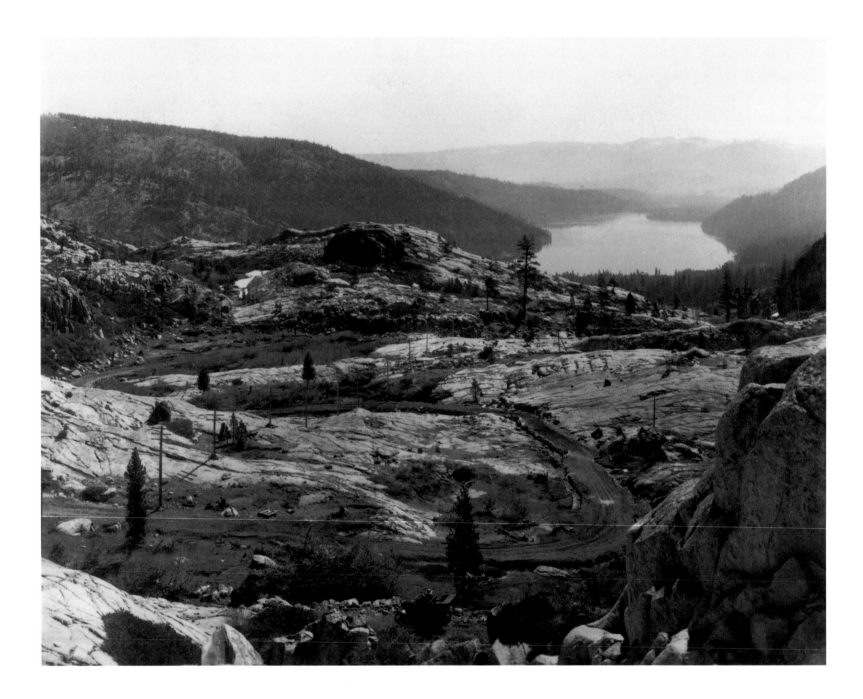

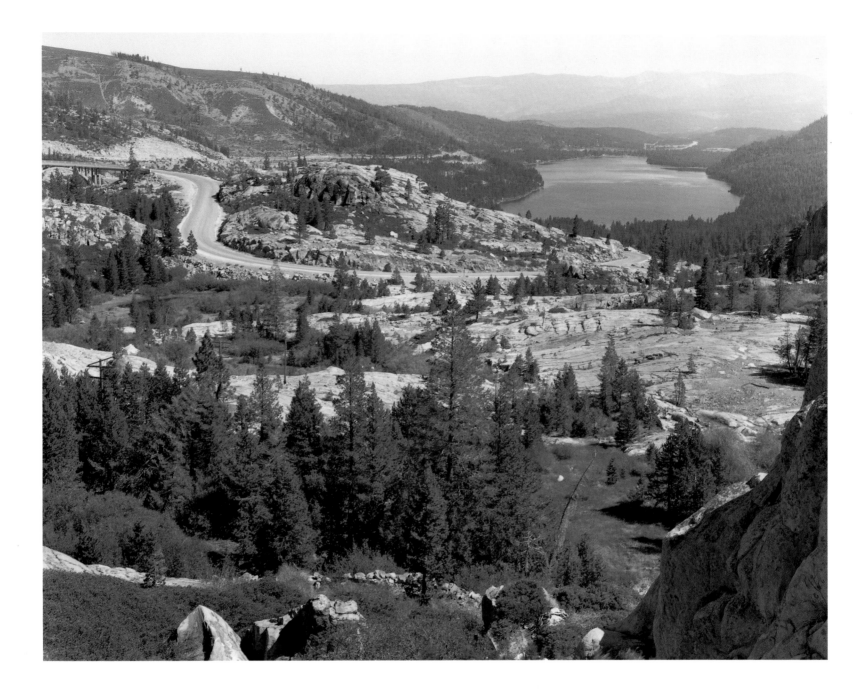

Donner Lake. This panoramic view from the west shows the old unpaved route over Donner Pass, now replaced by the bridge and pavement of the modern road. The woman in the car, located at the bottom of the early twentieth-century image by C. O. Valentine (left), sits patiently waiting for the photographer to complete the "best general view." The road along the east face of Donner Pass was significantly realigned in 1923, which led to rapid development of the area as a vacation resort and winter sports site. Here, too, there has been significant regrowth of the forest; note the scar from modern Interstate Highway 80, located along the ridge to the left of Donner Lake.

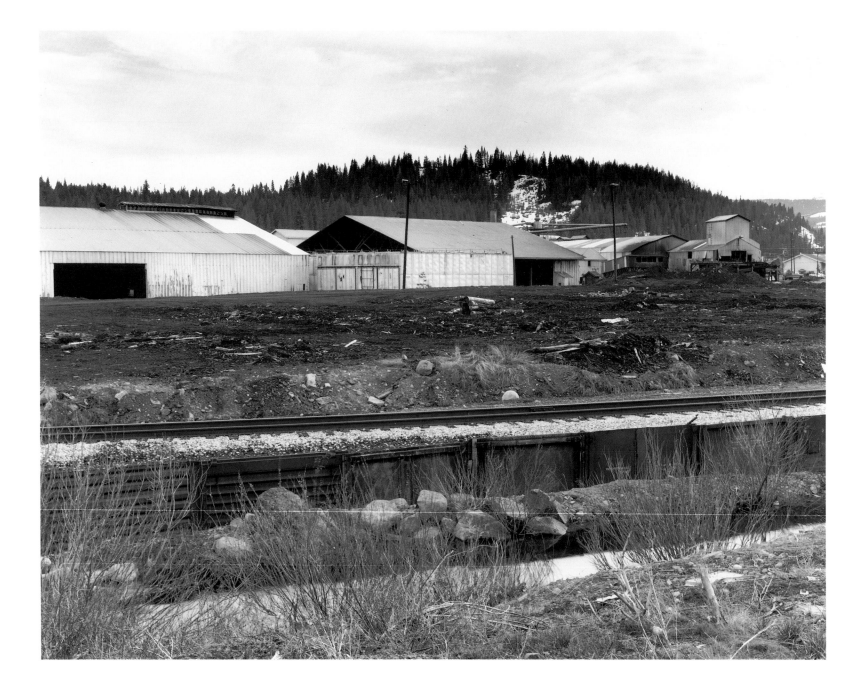

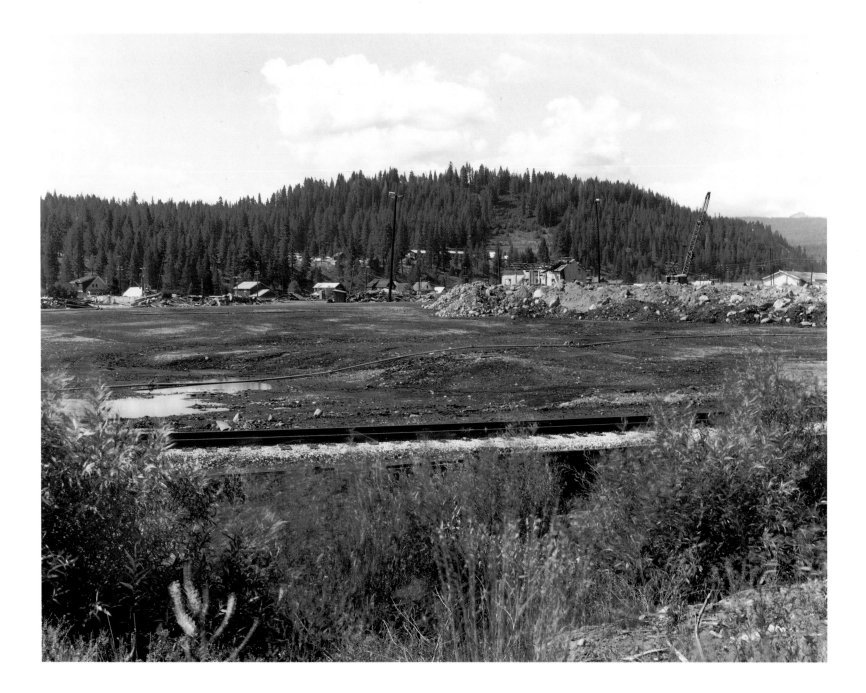

Truckee. The end of an era in the Tahoe basin: timber processing at Truckee finally ceased and the mill was removed in 1990. These two photographs were made only a few months apart.

The Historical Photographs

Robert E. Blesse

The quest for the historical photographs used in the Lake Tahoe Rephotographic Project took us to repositories throughout California and Nevada. Images came from both private collections and public repositories, small historical societies and large libraries. There was great interest shown by all who learned about the project and much cooperation from those who assisted in locating and providing images.

Interestingly enough, some of the major repositories consulted did not have as many photographs as might have been expected. In some of these cases, however, there simply was not adequate access to potentially valuable images of the lake that are probably in their collections. As is the case even in my own repository, providing complete subject access to tens of thousands of photographs is a costly, time-consuming, and often overwhelming undertaking. A substantial number of images of the Lake Tahoe region were found at the California Historical Society Library in San Francisco. Unfortunately these images were not available for reproduction due to the many problems that CHS is currently facing.

Early photographs of Lake Tahoe from the 1860s and 1870s were difficult to find. During this period, most of the activity at the lake was commercial, predominantly lumbering. Although the beauty of the lake and its surrounding region was recognized early on; it wasn't until tourists began to visit the area with some regularity that abundant commercial images were produced. We

were, however, pleased with the overall quality of images we were able to locate for this book. We found hundreds of excellent pictures in our research, and we certainly could have used two or three times as many as we did.

A number of the photographs in this book are well known, though many of them have not been published before. Individuals knowledgeable about California history are probably familiar with the photographs of Putnam and Valentine, a Los Angeles photography firm (1870s–1930s) that specialized in picturesque images of the West, particularly California. Included are photographs taken by both John Putnam and C. O. Valentine, who often included his wife in the scenic view. Both the North Lake Tahoe Historical Society and the Seaver Center at the Los Angeles County Museum of Natural History provided excellent images from this studio. The Pillsbury Photographic Company is another well-known studio which sold images of the lake, and historical photo buffs will be acquainted with the work of R. J. Waters, a Berkeley photographer prominent in the late nineteenth century. Carleton Watkins was one of the West's most important nineteenth-century photographers; he spent time at the lake making pictures, especially on the east shore around the Glenbrook area.

An excellent group of relatively unknown images are those from the Michael T. Benning Collection at the Sacramento Archives and Museum Collection Center. Benning was a commercial photographer from Sacramento who made a living specializing in photographs of school children and their classes in central California and Nevada. He had property in Kings Beach on the north shore of Lake Tahoe and spent his summers there, eventually opening Benning's Resort. He was also interested in documenting the Tahoe region. His extraordinary collection of Lake Tahoe photographs spans a period of over thirty years and includes pictures of resorts, towns, recreation areas, and, of course, the lake itself. Another valuable archive is the McCurry collection at the California Department of Transportation in Sacramento. A survey in itself, these images from the 1920s show the entire road around the California side of the lake.

We received considerable assistance and cooperation from many individuals and organizations. We were given access to many private collections, and I received professional courtesy from many colleagues at repositories throughout the state. Reno native Dr. James R. Herz made his entire collection of Tahoe photographs available to us, including many pristine images taken by Carleton Watkins. Jim is now graciously in the process of donating his extensive collection of photographs of Nevada and the West to the Special Collections Department at the University of Nevada, Reno Library. Another Nevada resident, William W. Bliss, provided photographs from his collection. The Bliss name is well known in the Tahoe region going back to his great-grandfather Duane L. Bliss, who was involved with logging and railroads in the Tahoe basin along with having extensive land holdings.

Long-time Tahoe resident Miriam Biro of the North Lake Tahoe Historical Society provided us with albums of photographs by Pillsbury and Putnam and Valentine. Gary Kurutz and his always helpful staff in the California Section of the California State Library provided assistance and a number of important photographs. Also in Sacramento, Charlene Gilbert of the Sacramento Archives and Museum Collection Center gave us use of the Michael T. Benning Collection, and Mary Hanel of the California Department of Transportation Library unearthed some real treasures, including the McCurry Collection. Finally, John Cahoon of the Seaver Center, Los Angeles County Museum of Natural History, assisted us with their extensive archive of images by Putnam and Valentine.

Acknowledgments

Without the assistance of the following people and institutions, this project might never have been completed: Dennis Albrecht, Dana Asbury, Miriam Biro, William W. Bliss, Jeff Bloch, John Cahoon, California Department of Transportation, California State Library, Linda Cole, Carol Cunningham, Stephen Davis, Karen Gash, Charlene Gilbert, Kari and Dana Goin, Robert Gorrell, Elizabeth Hadas, Mary Hanel, Dr. James Herz, Therese Heyman, Barbara Hitchcock, Gary Kurutz, Ed Laine, Mike Lanney, Susan Mantle, Chelsea Miller, Nevada Historical Society, North Lake Tahoe Historical Society, Linda Perry, Reed Powers, Jeff Reiner, Kathi Rick, Carol Robinson, Joe Rodino, Sacramento Archives & Museum Collection Center, Susan Searcy, Seaver Center at the Los Angeles County Museum of Natural History, South Lake Tahoe Chamber of Commerce, South Lake Tahoe Historical Society and Museum, Special Collections at the University of Nevada at Reno, Albert Todd, Kathryn Totton, Bob Truro, and the U.S. Forest Service Lake Tahoe Basin Management Unit.

This project was partially funded by the Sierra Arts Foundation, Reno, Nevada and through a Photographers' Materials Grant from the Polaroid Foundation. The Nevada Humanities Committee is traveling a selection of the photographs.

Kathi Rick produced the contemporary map of Lake Tahoe. As part of her internship in photography at the University of Nevada, Reno, Susan Mantle devoted considerable, time, skill, and energy producing the prints for fieldwork and publication. She produced the rephotographs on pages 55, 63, 128, and 129. Steve Davis produced the rephotograph on page 67.

Picture Credits

The numbers following the repository are page numbers where the item appears in this book.

Bancroft Library, University of California, Berkeley, *vii*

William Bliss Collection, *6, 38*

California Department of Transportation, Sacramento, *64, 84, 94*

California Section, California State Library, Sacramento, *3, 4, 28 bottom, 30, 52, 62, 88, 118, 120, 122*

Dr. James Herz Collection, *26, 36, 40, 58, 60, 102*

Nevada Historical Society, Reno, *56, 80, 96, 106, 108, 112 top*

North Lake Tahoe Historical Society, Tahoe City, *5 left, 45, 46, 50, 68, 70, 72, 74, 78, 82, 86, 92, 114, 126*

Sacramento Archives and Museum Collection Center, *98, 100, 101, 104, 106, 116*

Seaver Center for Western History, Los Angeles County Museum of Natural History, *32 top, 42, 54, 76, 90, 110*

South Lake Tahoe Historical Society, South Lake Tahoe, *34, 67*

Special Collections, Getchell Library, University of Nevada, Reno, *28 top, 44, 48, 124*